W9-BOM-710

SINGAPORE

ENCOUNTER

MAT OAKLEY

Singapore Encounter

Published by Lonely Planet Publications Pty Ltd
ABN 36 005 607 983

Australia	Head Office, Locked Bag 1, Footscray, Vic 3011 ☎ 03 8379 8000 fax 03 8379 8111 talk2us@lonelyplanet.com.au
USA	150 Linden St, Oakland, CA 94607 ☎ 510 250 6400 toll free 800 275 8555 fax 510 893 8572 info@lonelyplanet.com
UK	2nd fl, 186 City Rd London EC1V 2NT ☎ 020 7106 2100 fax 020 7106 2101 go@lonelyplanet.co.uk

This title was commissioned in Lonely Planet's Melbourne office and produced by: **Commissioning Editor** Holly Alexander **Coordinating Editor** Shawn Low **Coordinating Cartographer** Jacqueline Nguyen **Coordinating Layout Designer** Yvonne Bischofberger **Managing Editors** Melanie Dankel, Sasha Baskett **Managing Cartographer** David Connolly **Assisting Editor** Victoria Harrison **Assisting Layout Designer** Margie Jung **Cover Designer** Pepi Bluck **Project Managers** Glenn van der Knijff, Debra Herrmann **Series Designers** Mik Ruff, Wendy Wright **Managing Layout Designer** Celia Wood **Thanks to** Glenn Beanland, Diana Duggan, Nicole Hansen, Laura Jane, Indra Kilfoyle, Adam McCrow, Wayne Murphy, Naomi Parker

Cover photograph Buddha Tooth Relic Temple, Chinatown, Singapore, Felix Hug/Lonely Planet Images; **Internal photographs** p45, p63, p72, p95, p109, p139 by Mat Oakley; All other photographs by Lonely Planet Images and by Felix Hug except p24 Alain Evrard and p26 Susan Storm.

All images are copyright of the photographers unless otherwise indicated. Many of the images in this guide are available for licensing from **Lonely Planet Images:** www.lonelyplanetimages.com.

ISBN 978 1 74104 884 1

Printed by Hang Tai Printing Company, China.

Lonely Planet and the Lonely Planet logo are trademarks of Lonely Planet and are registered in the US Patent and Trademark Office and in other countries.

Lonely Planet does not allow its name or logo to be appropriated by commercial establishments, such as retailers, restaurants or hotels. Please let us know of any misuses: www.lonelyplanet.com/ip.

© Lonely Planet 2008. All rights reserved.

HOW TO USE THIS BOOK
Colour-Coding & Maps

Colour-coding is used for symbols on maps and in the text that they relate to (eg all eating venues on the maps and in the text are given a green knife and fork symbol). Each neighbourhood also gets its own colour, and this is used down the edge of the page and throughout that neighbourhood section.

Prices

Multiple prices listed with reviews (eg €10/5 or €10/5/20) indicate adult/child, adult/concession or adult/child/family.

Although the authors and Lonely Planet have taken all reasonable care in preparing this book, we make no warranty about the accuracy or completeness of its content and, to the maximum extent permitted, disclaim all liability arising from its use.

Send us your feedback We love to hear from readers — your comments help make our books better. We read every word you send us, and we always guarantee that your feedback goes straight to the appropriate authors. The most useful submissions are rewarded with a free book. To send us your updates and find out about Lonely Planet events, newsletters and travel news visit our award-winning website: *www.lonelyplanet.com/contact*.

Note: We may edit, reproduce and incorporate your comments in Lonely Planet products such as guidebooks, websites and digital products, so let us know if you don't want your comments reproduced or your name acknowledged. For a copy of our privacy policy visit *www.lonelyplanet.com/privacy*.

MAT OAKLEY

Son of a Scouse git, Mat grew up in Watford, and to this day still struggles to understand what his parents saw in the place. Since leaving England in the early '90s, he has lived in Thailand, Laos, Australia and Fiji, working for newspapers, news agencies and as a freelance writer. Since 2004 he has been living in Singapore with his wife, two misbehaving Fijian cats and an interloping local feline. In between efforts to avoid becoming yet another motorcycle victim of the city's psychotic drivers, he enjoys discovering another place to

eat, visiting another microbrewery whose products need lengthy evaluation, seeking out Singapore's oases of greenery and heaping abuse on Manchester United.

MAT'S THANKS

Thanks to Tracy Gan, Rosalyn Lim, Vanessa Frida and Andrew Duffy for their eating and drinking tips, and to Rishad Patel, Shefali Srinivas and Alan Grant for helping test some of those places. Cheers to my dad, who uncomplainingly spent holiday time trudging around the streets and to little Mae for testing the kids' attractions. Lastly to Shiwani, who makes everything worthwhile.

THE PHOTOGRAPHER

Felix Hug used to shoot hoops for a professional basketball team in Switzerland before he decided that shooting images was more enjoyable. In 2007, Felix was the runner-up at the Travel Photographer of the Year awards. He received an honourable mention at the *PDN/National Geographic Traveler* 'World in Focus' contest in 2005 and took home the *Asian Geographic* Nikon Grand Prize in 2004. Felix believes that the job of the travel photographer is to capture inspiring images instead of just documenting reality: 'Positive images and compassion will inspire and change the way we look at things.'

Our readers Many thanks to the travellers who wrote to us with helpful hints, useful advice and interesting anecdotes. Thomas Bosch, Rami Giron, Ilsa Hampton, Michelle Imison, Eve Montgomery, SB Tan, Nghia Trong, Graeme Wooler, Joanna Yates

Laid-back Clarke Quay comes alive at night thanks to an assortment of bars, clubs and restaurants

CONTENTS

Our authors are independent, dedicated travellers. They don't research using just the internet or phone, and they don't take freebies, so you can rely on their advice being well researched and impartial. They travel widely, visiting thousands of places, taking great pride in getting all the details right and telling it how it is.

THIS IS SINGAPORE

Once sullenly wary of outsiders, Singapore is now screaming its name to world. Once upon a time they stopped longhairs at the border, now they're offering them big salaries to run digital animation labs. Once upon a time the city frowned on late nights, alcohol and wanton frivolity, now it's one of the nightlife capitals of Asia.

Once upon a time in Singapore... The fairy tales still get told of social controls so obsessively, surreally punctilious they achieved global infamy. Yes, it's still illegal to chew gum (without prescription!) and jaywalk, and yes the government still fusses, prods and badgers its citizens in every single aspect of their lives, but the 'Fine' city has actually transcended the joke and become, yes, a fine city.

At the centre of it all, the Colonial District is its cultural heart, home to some of Asia's most outstanding museums, some of its grandest Victorian architecture and, providing a spiky counterpoint, the unforgettable Esplanade theatre overlooking Marina Bay. Singapore's economic lifeblood used to flow through that bay and up the river. Now the shadow of a new economy looms over it, as the giant Sands casino resort rises towards completion, while a barrage has turned the bay into a reservoir that will be the centrepiece for the New Singapore: globally minded, affluent and fun.

Upstream, echoes of the past cling to the river bank, but the belch and clatter of bumboat commerce has given way to the belch and clatter of drinkers and diners, as business people mingle with mall-weary tourists over a few sundowners before taking on some of the city's superb clubs and restaurants. And everywhere, from fancy French cuisine to the ubiquitous hawker stalls, is food, the one defining obsession that unites everyone, if only momentarily. Any visitor willing to throw themselves into this food paradise will find no quicker way into the soul of Singapore.

Top Another exciting night of live music (p165) in Singapore **Bottom** Watch the Singapore skyline slowly roll by from the cabin of the Singapore Flyer (p73)

>HIGHLIGHTS

The National Museum of Singapore (p70) at dusk – a stunning sight to behold

>1 LITTLE INDIA

A SLICE OF THE SUBCONTINENT A STONE'S THROW FROM THE MALLS

Many parts of Singapore have been trampled by shopping centres – a process of mall-ification that has robbed entire areas of their sense of place. Little India is one of the happy exceptions and for our money there is nowhere in Singapore that matches it for street atmosphere, especially at night.

Little India teems with life – it's hard to believe you're just a few minutes from Orchard Rd – and the greatest pleasure is wandering around to soak it all up: the countless places to eat, the gold shops filled with haggling families from India, the garland sellers, CD shops thumping bhangra and the dozens of smells, both good and bad. While many areas of the city die after dark, there always seems to be activity on the streets of Little India, which light up spectacularly in October for the Deepavali festival.

Serangoon Rd forms the spine of the district, but it's the lanes on either side that warrant the most exploring. Next to the pungent wet market, hawker centre and 1st-floor sari shops of Tekka Market (p90), Buffalo Rd's open-air vegetable stalls bustle around the clock, spilling detritus onto the street as shoppers shuffle along the five-foot-ways lined with bags plump with okra, eggplants and more. There's something refreshingly grubby and un-Singaporean about it all.

Race Course Rd is thick with food shops, including the famous Banana Leaf Apolo (p92), where diners sweat over fiery fish-head curry every night. Around the Dunlop St and Dickson Rd area are more eateries, handicraft shops, hostels and the Prince of Wales pub (p94).

At the other end of Serangoon Rd is the notorious Mustafa Centre (p89), a 24-hour shopping behemoth crammed with every known retailable item on earth and, it sometimes seems, every person too.

>2 CHINATOWN

TAKE A STROLL AMONG THE SHOPHOUSES

It might seem strange to have a Chinatown in a city dominated by ethnic Chinese, but this district of narrow lanes and once-crumbling shophouses was the area Sir Stamford Raffles demarcated in his segregated Singapore town plan for the Chinese immigrants.

The area is still rich in history – and the first stop for any new visitor should be the Chinatown Heritage Centre (p51), which portrays the district's squalid past. It's hard to imagine, now that the renovators have swarmed all over the place and filled it with boutique hotels and fashionable restaurants. Pockets of old Chinatown still remain in streets such as Keong Saik Rd and Chinatown Complex.

Pagoda, Temple, Smith and Trengganu Sts are the tourist traps, riddled with market stalls (and a great night food market) and bookended by two important religious sites: the Hindu Sri Mariamman Temple (p51) and newly built Buddha Tooth Relic Temple (p51).

Cross South Bridge Rd and enter Club St, once home to many clan association headquarters, now magnet for fashionable businesses and restaurants. Over the top of Ann Siang Hill are Amoy and Telok Ayer Sts, home of the Thian Hock Keng temple (p54), an area that heaves with lunching office workers during the day, but is almost deserted at night.

>3 ORCHARD ROAD
PAY HOMAGE TO THE GODS OF RETAIL

Orchard Rd was once a leafy boulevard lined with plantations (hence the name). These days, though, Singapore's money doesn't grow on trees; it's harvested in malls – and nowhere do they grow more thickly than here. The sheer scale of this retail barrage can be oppressive and overwhelming, particularly for reluctant shoppers (in other words, men). On weekends and in holiday seasons, the pavements are often so packed that walking is reduced to a shuffle. But there are compensations for those who contemplate with horror a day of gasping at shoes and suffering lathers of indecision over dresses – including the street's many wonderful opportunities for eating and, if you're there during Christmas, the breathtaking light displays.

Orchard Rd and its environs encompass many miniature worlds. Observe the expat wives comparing maid problems over cake at Tanglin Mall (p42) or Paragon (p42), teen fashion molls evaluating the latest Japanese pink fur boots at Far East Plaza (p42), hipsters calculating the cool quotient of a $90 T-shirt at the Heeren (p42), hopeful European men eyeing up the parades of Thai and Filipina girls at Orchard Towers, hopeful Indian men eyeing up the maids who congregate in their thousands at Lucky Plaza on Sundays, or the fussy, bouffanted *tai-tais* (wealthy ladies of leisure) bothering the perfume girls at posh Takashimaya (p42).

>4 ZOO & NIGHT SAFARI
CLOSE ENCOUNTERS OF THE FURRED KIND

Sometimes the relentless development and redevelopment of Singapore can become tiresome, but not in the case of its world-class zoo and Night Safari (p48), which are forever being upgraded and always for the better. Whatever your opinion of zoos, it can't be denied that the Singapore Zoo has made an excellent job of keeping its animals as happy as possible.

The first creatures you encounter are free-ranging primates: cottontop tamarins, white-faced sakis and siamangs – and there are few places outside Borneo and Sumatra where you can stand under trees with orang-utans a few feet above your head.

Other highlights include the Fragile Forest, a large dome where lemurs and mouse deer scamper across your path, a tree kangaroo lazes in the branches and large flying foxes munch fruit in front of your face.

As evening closes in, the Night Safari next door to the zoo uses open-concept enclosures to get visitors up close with nocturnal creatures such as leopards, free-ranging deer and Malayan tiger.

>5 HAWKER STALLS
FOOD HEAVEN UNDER FLUORO LIGHTS

It is one of the great pleasures of Singapore: ambling into a bustling hawker centre in your flip-flops, picking out a table, wandering among the steam and smoke and chatter of the stalls, then settling down with a few cold beers and stuffing your face. And since almost everything is signed in English, Singapore is one of the most accessible places in Asia to dive into a massive range of regional cuisine.

The traditional favourite for visitors is Newton Circus (p46), which specialises in great seafood, but the touting here can be aggressive. The historical Lau Pa Sat Festival Market (p58) in the CBD is a must-visit – it's recently been 'upgraded' to 'tourist standard' and many would argue its charm has been lost. In Chinatown, the Smith St Hawker Centre (p61) is a treat, while the Maxwell Rd Hawker Centre (p59) further down the road has a much more local flavour. For a real taste of old-time hawker food where few tourists ever visit, head for Hong Lim Complex (p58) in Chinatown.

For seaside eats, the East Coast Lagoon Food Village (p107) is well-known for its satay stalls and it heaves at night – the perfect spot for a meal and a postprandial stroll along the seashore.

>6 HIGH DINING
WHATEVER YOU FANCY

For many years, Singapore has been in a pitched battle with other countries in the region to cast itself as the food capital of Asia, promoting not only its vibrant (if sometimes sanitised) hawker culture but also its high-end restaurants. There is certainly no shortage of options to lighten your wallet in the name of fine dining, but while the food is frequently top-notch, it has to be said the service in Singapore can leave much to be desired.

Top of the pile for food, service and atmosphere is probably Au Jardin Les Amis (p123) in the Botanic Gardens. Club St also houses several excellent European restaurants, notably L'Angelus (p58) and Senso (p60), while Holland Village's Jalan Merah Saga also contains fine European restaurants such as Original Sin (p124). For fancy Chinese food, locals usually head for big-name restaurants such as Shang Palace (p46) or Royal China (p75), while expat Japanese in Singapore barrel down to Cuppage Plaza for the best taste of home.

>7 SINGAPORE BOTANIC GARDENS

A BREATH OF FRESH AIR

Like all great urban green spaces, entering Singapore's Botanic
Gardens (p117) provides instant relief: the roar of traffic melts into
the branches and it's easy to forget that you're surrounded by 4.5
million people.

And like most things in Singapore, it's immaculate and well-
designed. Each area segues into the next, each with its own atmosphere, from the lazy serenity of the Swan Lake to the dense, humid
greenery of the rainforest zone, to the carefully pruned bonsai and
orchid gardens: careful landscaping sits side by side with huge old
trees that first poked their heads above ground when Queen Victoria
was surveying her Empire.

Of course, visitors don't go hungry. Just inside the Tanglin Gate is a
large food court, while the gardens themselves host two of the city's
most irresistibly romantic restaurants: Au Jardin Les Amis (p123) and
Halia (p123).

Check out the gardens' listing of upcoming events for free tours
and the regular free outdoor classical concerts that take place on the
Symphony Stage.

>8 RAFFLES HOTEL
SPEND SUNSET WITH SOMERSET

Yes, yes, it's a cliché, but it's also hard to resist the allure of that magnificent ivory frontage, the famous Sikh doorman, the colonial elegance and the echoes of Maugham and Conrad and the days when Singapore was a swampy, dissolute outpost of the British Empire.

Raffles Hotel (p71) started life in 1887 as a modest 10-room bungalow built by the Armenian Sarkies brothers, a far cry from the global brand it has become now, when far more people visit it than sleep in it.

It's best visited in the late afternoon or early evening, when the heat has been sapped from the day, the spotlights bathe the building in romance and the tourists are slightly thinner on the ground, perhaps decanting themselves into the hotel's bars and restaurants.

The Raffles Museum is well-worth half an hour. Steer clear of the too-famous Long Bar and slip into a veranda chair at the far more atmospheric Bar & Billiard Room (p76) for an early evening aperitif, followed by one of the best buffets in the city: the incredible, stomach-popping Indian feast laid on nightly in the Tiffin Room (p75).

>9 MUSEUMS
SINGAPORE IN THE PAST TENSE

Singapore hosts some of the finest museums in Southeast Asia – enough to take a week to explore, let alone the average two or three days most visitors spend here. Most of the best ones are concentrated in the city centre, which makes it easy to hop between them.

Joint favourite is the grand Asian Civilisations Museum (p67), whose second branch on Armenian St was being converted, at the time of writing, into the Peranakan Museum. The National Museum of Singapore (p70), housed in an architecturally superb Victorian building and modern annex, is equally magnificent. Close by is the recently refurbished Singapore Art Museum (p71).

WWII and the Japanese occupation had an enormous impact on the city, and the experience has been preserved in many laudable museums: Fort Siloso on Sentosa (p98), the Battle Box at Fort Canning Park (p39), Kent Ridge Park's Reflections At Bukit Chandu (p132) commemorating the Malay Regiment's resistance, Labrador Park's secret tunnels (p129), the Old Ford Factory (p117) where the British surrendered, the moving POW memorial at Changi Memorial & Chapel (p106) and the heartbreaking Kranji War Memorial (p177). There are also several memorials around the island, including the site of a Japanese massacre of Chinese civilians at Changi Beach Park.

>10 SENTOSA
SURRENDER TO A WORLD OF ILLUSION

Once a byword for tackiness, Singapore's pleasure isle has been – and continues to be – reborn. Those same blistering beaches of imported sand are still lapped by the oily ocean and thinly shaded by trucked-in palm trees, but the entertainment and eating options are much better than they used to be and the island is about to place itself on the world tourism map with the vast new Resorts World hotel-casino, which is set to open in 2010 and will house a Universal Studios Theme Park.

A new monorail feeds the island with visitors, though many still prefer the dizzy ride on the cable car, not least because it dumps them straight at the addictive Sentosa Luge & Skyride (p103), an all-too-short chance to race your friends down to the beach in a vehicle that looks like a baby bath on wheels.

Sun-lovers can plonk themselves under a palm tree, or at one of the Ibiza-inspired bar restaurants such as Café del Mar (p101), KM8 (p103) or Coastes (p100). The more energetic check out Underwater World (p100) and Dolphin Lagoon, while the revamped Images of Singapore (p98) museum is one of the city's better attempts at evoking its past, as is the war museum at Fort Siloso (p98).

As the sun sets and the city's weekend beach bunnies migrate to the bars to expose tanned flesh, the Songs of the Sea (p99) light-and-sound show entertains the less party-inclined.

>11 EAST COAST PARK

RECLAIM THE DAY

Seldom can reclaimed land have been put to such good use. East Coast Park stretches close to 11km and is one of Singapore's most pleasant urban escapes. It's only narrow, but has been superbly designed so that the landscape constantly shifts and changes and the bordering road rarely encroaches on the peace and quiet.

The park offers numerous opportunities for exercise: cycling and rollerblading, wakeboarding and waterskiing at the Ski 360° (p113) lagoon, and windsurfing and sailing.

Cycling from the western end to the eastern end, where the planes coming in to land at Changi airport roar directly overhead, and marvelling at the sheer number of ships that anchor offshore is a great way to spend a weekday. During weekends, though, it's too packed to be enjoyable.

And of course, it wouldn't be Singapore if there weren't dozens of places to eat and drink, ranging from the wildly popular No Signboard Seafood (p108) to the tiny Mango Tree (p108) Indian restaurant and the outdoor hawker centre at East Coast Lagoon Food Village (p107).

>12 BUKIT TIMAH & MACRITCHIE
TIPTOE PAST THE PYTHONS

If the Botanic Gardens are an admirable exercise in managed vegetation, then the area officially (and uninspiringly) known as the Central Catchment Area is a masterpiece of urban wilderness planning.

Bukit Timah Nature Reserve (p117), the highest point on the island at 163m, is one of only two patches of urban primary rainforest in the world (the other is in Rio de Janeiro). Though it has been laid with a concrete path, side trails plunge deep into a forest so rich that one botanist estimated there are more plant species there than in the whole of North America.

Linked to Bukit Timah is the MacRitchie Reservoir nature reserve, which is ringed with dozens of kilometres of trails (see Walking Tour p146), where walkers can spot macaques, monitor lizards, the occasional python and flying lemur – and walk across the Treetop Walk suspension bridge – before ending up at the peaceful reservoir park.

>SINGAPORE DIARY

Singapore's rich ethnic brew has resulted in a packed calendar of religious holidays and people of all creeds are encouraged by the city's multicultural masters to participate (though we presume they don't mind if you draw the line at putting skewers through your cheeks). Combine these with annual food, fashion, film, music and shopping events and it becomes pretty difficult to visit Singapore without encountering some festival or other. Before arriving, check the tourism board's excellent online events calendar (www.visitsingapore.com) for the latest.

Singapore is awash with lights and festivities during Chinese New Year (p24)

JANUARY

Ponggal

South Indian harvest festival in mid-January that's heralded with much noise-making — it's customary to cook sweet rice in a pot and let it boil over to symbolise bounty. Place to be: Little India or Sri Mariamman Temple (p51).

Thaipusam

Dramatic Hindu festival featuring acts of masochism. Devotees carry frames attached to their bodies with flesh-piercing skewers and hooks. Place to be: watching the procession from Serangoon Rd to Tank Rd.

FEBRUARY

Chinese New Year

The biggest holiday on the Singapore calendar, marked by lion dancing and brightly decorated trucks carrying drum- and cymbal-bashing men. Families hold open house, unmarried relatives receive *ang pow* (money in red packets) and businesses try to clear their debts. Place to be: Chinatown, of course!

Chingay

www.chingay.org.sg

Huge, vibrant annual street parade and party (usually with undercurrent themes reinforcing social order and racial harmony), held on the 22nd day after Chinese New Year. Formerly

The Chingay parade is a raucous riot of colour and sound

on Orchard Rd, but moved to Colonial District in 2008. Buy tickets for viewing galleries, or fight the crowds for vantage points.

MARCH

Singapore Fashion Festival

www.singaporefashionfestival.com.sg

Around 10 days of shows, promotions and general flouncing to showcase the work of local designers and prominent international names.

Mosaic Music Festival

www.mosaicmusicfestival.com

An annual 10-day feast of jazz, funk, hip-hop, world music etc in the Esplanade – Theatres on the Bay (p67). Many well-known acts perform and there are also free concerts.

APRIL

Qing Ming Festival

Often called All Souls Day, this is when Chinese show gratitude and respect to their ancestors by cleaning and repairing their tombs (or, these days, more likely their urns at the columbarium) and making offerings. Place to be: Kong Meng San Phor Kark See Monastery.

Singapore International Film Festival

www.filmfest.org.sg

Independent and art-house movies are pretty thin on the ground in Hollywood-obsessed Singapore, so this usually excellent festival of world cinema is a rare treat.

World Gourmet Summit

www.worldgourmetsummit.com

Annual gathering of top chefs and celebrities for an orgy of dinners and brunches in the city's top restaurants, as well as wine tastings and cooking master classes.

MAY

Vesak Day

Celebration of Buddha's birth, enlightenment and death through various events, including the releasing of caged birds or other animals to symbolise setting souls free (a practice now actively discouraged since the helpless creatures usually die in the wild). Places to be: Sakaya Muni Buddha Gaya Temple or Buddha Tooth Relic Temple (p51).

JUNE

Great Singapore Sale

www.greatsingaporesale.com

Running from the end of May to the beginning of July (it seems to get longer every year), Orchard Rd and malls are decked with banners, and retailers slash prices. Shoppers' paradise or tourist-board gimmick? Opinions are divided.

Dragon Boat Festival

www.sdba.org.sg

A frenzy of paddling on the Bedok Reservoir in Eastern Singapore. Other dragon-boat events are held throughout the year, including the Singapore River Regatta in November.

Singapore Arts Festival

www.singaporeartsfest.com

Starting in late May and ending in late June, this annual showcase features local and international dance, music and theatre.

JULY

Singapore Food Festival

www.singaporefoodfestival.com

A month-long celebration of all things edible and Singaporean. Well-known restaurants

lay on events and there are cooking classes, food-themed tours for visitors and plenty of opportunities to sample classic Malay, Chinese and Indian dishes.

AUGUST

National Day

www.ndp.org.sg

Held on 9 August (rehearsals on the two prior weekends are popular), this huge nationalist frenzy takes all year to prepare and showcases military parades, extravagant civilian processions, air-force flybys, frenzied flag-waving and a concluding fireworks display. Look out for the rows of white-clad People's Action Party (PAP) members.

Hungry Ghost Festival

Day when the souls of the dead are released for feasting and entertainment on Earth. Place to be: Chinatown, but look for food offerings left out for the spirits all over the city.

Womad

www.womadsingapore.com

Festival of world music at Fort Canning Park marking the end of the two-week National Day celebrations. Don't worry, it's not all pan pipes and Celtic ankle flutes.

SEPTEMBER

Mooncake Festival

Also known as the Lantern Festival. Sample the namesake cake – traditionally made

Chinese opera at the Hungry Ghost Festival

The spectacular Thimithi fire-walking ceremony at the Sri Mariamman Temple

with bean paste and duck-egg filling, nowadays mooncakes come in all flavours.

Formula 1 Grand Prix
www.f1singapore.com
Whether this becomes an annual event depends on the success of the first one – F1's first-ever night race – in September 2008. Knowing Singapore, it'll go like clockwork.

OCTOBER

Deepavali
The Hindu Festival of Lights sees Little India illuminated by a huge light display for the entire month and a big street party on the eve of the day itself.

Hari Raya Puasa
Also known as Hari Raya Aidilfitri, this festival celebrates the end of the Ramadan fasting month (it can also occur in September). Place to be: the Arab Quarter for nightly feasts during Ramadan.

NOVEMBER

Thimithi
The mildly frenzied, often raucous Hindu fire-walking festival, when men stroll

PILGRIMAGE TO KUSU

Kusu Island, which means 'Tortoise Island' in Chinese, is normally a tranquil pocket of partly reclaimed land in the Singapore Strait and dotted with trees, picnic benches and small beaches. It houses an attractive Taoist temple to Da Bo Gong (God of Prosperity) and Guan Yin (Goddess of Mercy) and, on top of a prominent central hill, three Malay *kramats* (shrines to saints).

But every year, in the ninth month of the Chinese lunar calendar (some time between late September and November), the island is deluged at weekends with thousands of people, who come to the island on a pilgrimage to pray for wealth, health and good fortune.

According to legend, a magical tortoise spied two drowning sailors – one Malay and one Chinese – and turned itself into an island to save them.

Boats to Kusu, for the time being, leave from Marina South Pier (Map pp52–3, H3) at 10am and 2pm Monday to Friday; 9am, noon and 3pm Saturday; 9am, 11am, 1pm, 3pm and 5pm Sunday.

across white-hot coals to demonstrate faith. Place to be: Sri Mariamman Temple (p51).

Singapore Buskers' Festival

It all feels a little forced, but this showcase of street-performing talent succeeds in injecting colour and life into Singapore's streets. Places to be: Orchard Rd and the Quays.

DECEMBER

Christmas

Celebrated with a predictable consumerist frenzy, which, as elsewhere, seems to start several months beforehand. Singapore's

Christmas is notable for the breathtaking light display (and not so breathtaking displays of giant Santas, house-sized presents and suchlike) that stretches the entire length of Orchard Rd. The light-up ceremony is in mid-November.

Hari Raya Haji

An event celebrating the conclusion of the pilgrimage to Mecca. Animals (mostly sheep) are ritually slaughtered in the mosques, after which the *Koran* dictates a portion of the meat must be handed out to the poor. The event will take place in November in 2009, 2010 and 2011.

The view of Singapore's soaring CBD skyline from Cavenagh Bridge

ITINERARIES

Singapore, unlike many cities, doesn't impose geographic restrictions on your day; it's just 40 minutes in a taxi between opposite corners of the island. It's perfectly feasible to spend a morning on Sentosa and an afternoon on Pulau Ubin. And despite the energy-sapping climate, you're usually never too far from a refreshing breeze or blissful dose of air-conditioning.

DAY ONE

Start with a stroll through the Singapore Botanic Gardens (p117), followed by eats and coffee at Halia (p123). Catch a bus to Orchard Rd and spend a few hours in retail heaven – or hell (see the boxed text, p42). Have lunch at Food Republic (p44), pick up some treats at the Takashimaya basement, then head for the National Museum of Singapore (p70). Afterwards, take the back exit, walk through Fort Canning Park (p39), then past Parliament to the Asian Civilisations Museum (p67). Have dinner by the bay at the Pierside Kitchen & Bar (p75), then either stroll to the Swissôtel, The Stamford and up 70 floors for quiet drinks at City Space (p76), or head for the noisier nightlife of Clarke Quay for a dance at Cuba Libre (p76).

DAY TWO

Take the MRT to Little India (p82) and spend the morning shopping and temple-spotting. Stop for lunch at Gayatri (p92) or Tekka Centre (p93), then take a cab to the Singapore Zoo (p48) for the afternoon. If you don't feel like staying for the Night Safari (p48), go back to Raffles Hotel in town for a few tipples at the Bar & Billiard Room (p76), then cab it up to Arab St for a Middle Eastern feast and a *shisha* (flavoured tobacco smoked in a hookah), followed by drinks at BluJaz Café (p94).

DAY THREE

Begin the day in the leafy heights of Mt Faber Park (p129), before taking the cable car across to Sentosa Island (p96). Hop off and race across the road for a few runs on the Sentosa Luge (p103). Find a spot for a laze on the beach then have lunch at Coastes (p100). Walk down the beach to

Top left Singapore's latest club, St James Power Station (p134) **Top right** Families will enjoy riding on the Skyride (p103) on Sentosa **Bottom** A replica statue of David in the rotunda at the National Museum of Singapore (p70)

Fort Siloso (p98), visit Underwater World (p100), if it's not too crowded, then take in the Songs of the Sea (p99) show. Afterwards, nip across the bridge to Keppel Island for drinks and dinner by the water at Privé (p134), followed by a night out at the St James Power Station (p134).

DAY FOUR

You got bumped off your flight, so head for the Singapore Flyer (p73) for a quick spin. Then go to Changi Village and take a bumboat across to Pulau Ubin (p114) to spend the day cycling through the forest. Take a late lunch and a few beers at Season Live Seafood (p114), then head back to the 'mainland' and go to East Coast Park (Map p105, F3) to relax on the beach. Finish off with sea-front curry at the Mango Tree (p108).

Giraffes at Singapore Zoo (p48)

FORWARD PLANNING

Three weeks before you go Visit some of the Singapore websites (p192) and check out the Singapore Tourism Board online calendar for upcoming events. Book a table at Au Jardin Les Amis (p123) or if you prefer a Chinese feast, book at My Humble House (p75). Check to see if your visit coincides with any holidays or festivals (p23) – you might want your hotel to be close to (or far from) a celebration.

One week before you go Check for concerts at the Esplanade (p67) and book tickets. Check the Jazz@Southbridge (p80) and BluJaz Café (p94) websites for the following week's concerts. Read the *Straits Times'* Stomp website (www.stomp.com.sg) to get an idea of the day-to-day issues (just don't expect any political discussion).

One day before you go Check the Singapore Tourism calendar for last-minute updates. Buy Singapore dollars. Phone the cat sitter. Check the newspapers to make sure the government hasn't been overthrown in a coup.

RAINY DAY

Singapore is known for scorching sunshine and sudden, heavy downpours, so the city is designed for shelter. If it's pouring, head for the museums (p170), or explore the underground warren of shops inside the City Link Mall (Map pp68–9) – it's possible to spend half a day down there without ever poking your head above ground.

FOR FREE

Singapore Inc is not fond of offering its products for nothing, but there are ways to enjoy yourself, even if you've just lost your wallet. The Buddha Tooth Relic Temple & Museum (p51) is free to enter – and there's free vegetarian food in the basement. After that, a stroll through Fort Canning Park (p39) or Kent Ridge Park (p129) is a pleasant way to fill a couple of hours. If it's lunchtime, the Singapore Art Museum (p71) has free entry between noon and 2pm on weekdays, and from 6pm to 9pm Friday. The Esplanade (p67) also stages regular free Friday concerts and there are sometimes free classical concerts in the Singapore Botanic Gardens (p117). If evening is creeping close, next to Fort Canning Park is the National Museum of Singapore (p70), where the excellent Living Galleries are free between 6pm and 9pm.

The imposing gothic gate at Fort Canning Park (p39) was built in 1846

ITINERARIES

Girls preparing to perform an Indian dance

NEIGHBOURHOODS

The compact layout of Singapore's city centre and its excellent public-transport system make scooting between neighbourhoods easy, despite the wilting heat and occasional spectacular downpours. Even if you're walking, the city's abundant greenery often provides plenty of shade.

The ethnic enclaves Sir Stamford Raffles created with his original town plan resulted in sharply delineated districts that still exist in some form today. At the heart of it all is the Colonial District, hugging the mouth and the north bank of the Singapore River and brimming with elegant Victorian-era buildings, many (such as Raffles Hotel) which are icons of the city.

Spreading along the river are the thriving quays, home to countless waterside restaurants, pubs, bars and clubs, while west of the district, the Doric columns suddenly give way to the brash, towering edifices that line Orchard Rd, Singapore's famous shopping strip.

Head north from the Colonial District and the transformation is equally dramatic, as the sugar-white façade of the Raffles Hotel recedes and bustling Bugis St market passes by, the faces on the streets change and there is Little India, minutes away but a world apart. South of the river, beyond the dramatic thicket of CBD skyscrapers, lies Chinatown, home to both the tackiest side of the tourist trade and some of the coolest nightlife.

Leave the city heading east and things change again as the traditional Malay and Straits Chinese (Peranakan) districts of Geylang and Katong emerge, with streets lined with old tatty shophouses and dens of vice in Geylang, and the more decorous, dignified eating houses and restored buildings of Katong. Laid along the fringe of these two areas is the long ribbon of East Coast Park.

West of the city, past the sublime Botanic Gardens, are the affluent condominiums and landed properties of Holland Rd and Bukit Timah, hiding pockets of offbeat shops and fancy restaurants.

And lying off the coast to the south is Sentosa, Singapore's reborn fantasy island.

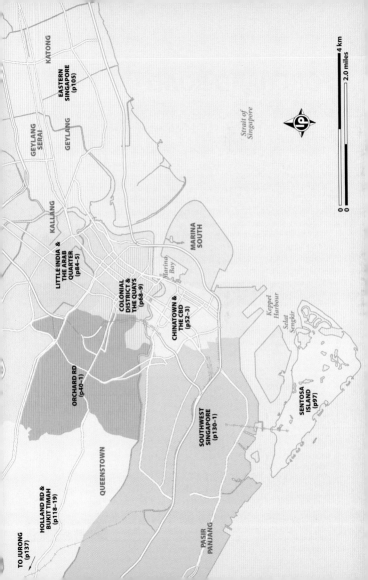

KATONG

EASTERN SINGAPORE (p105)

GEYLANG SERAI

GEYLANG

Strait of Singapore

KALLANG

MARINA SOUTH

LITTLE INDIA & THE ARAB QUARTER (p84–5)

Marina Bay

COLONIAL DISTRICT & THE QUAYS (p68–9)

CHINATOWN & THE CBD (p52–3)

Keppel Harbour

Selat Sengkir

ORCHARD RD (p40–1)

SENTOSA ISLAND (p97)

SOUTHWEST SINGAPORE (p130–1)

QUEENSTOWN

HOLLAND RD & BUKIT TIMAH (p118–19)

TO JURONG (p137)

PASIR PANJANG

0   2.0 miles

0   4 km

>ORCHARD ROAD

A veritable canyon of concrete, glass and steel, Orchard Rd is a monument to the Singaporean obsession with shopping, though it's really a chicken-and-egg proposition: did the obsession spawn the malls, or did the malls spawn the obsession?

Either way, Singaporeans love these monoliths, spending vast amounts of leisure time bathing in icy air-conditioning, shopping, eating, drinking and movie-going.

Orchard Rd is the Mecca for this retail religion. While a certain sameness has begun to creep into many malls – chain stores and restaurants colonise space, and high rents push out the small-timers – many shops, particularly the older ones, retain their ability to surprise.

It's not all shallow commercialism either. At the eastern end of Orchard are the hugely impressive National Museum of Singapore, Singapore Art Museum and the recently opened Peranakan Museum and looming over them is the blissful oasis of Fort Canning Park.

ORCHARD ROAD

Please see over for map

NEIGHBOURHOODS

ORCHARD ROAD

SEE

FORT CANNING PARK

Once you get over the climb up the stairs, Fort Canning is not only a wonderful hilltop retreat from the city filled with shady paths and hidden nooks, it's a fascinating historical site. Check out the huge fort doors, the former barracks building, the spice garden and The Battle Box museum.

THE BATTLE BOX

☎ 6333 0510; www.legendsfortcanning /fortcanning/battlebox.htm; 51 Canning Rise; adult/child $8/5; ☺ 10am-6pm; Ⓜ Dhoby Ghaut; ♿

Site of the former headquarters of the British Malaya Command, now a museum recreating the last hours before the fall of Singapore to the Japanese on 15 February, 1942, using reasonably lifelike

GETTING THERE & AROUND

> **MRT** – Orchard, Somerset and Dhoby Ghaut stations run west to east.
> **Bus** – 36, 124, 162, 174 and 518 run the length of the road.

wax figures and unsettling audio effects simulating the bombing.

SHOP

KINOKUNIYA *Bookshop*

☎ 6737 5021; 03-09/15, Ngee Ann City, 391 Orchard Rd; ☺ 10.30am-9.30pm Sun-Fri, 10am-10pm Sat; Ⓜ Orchard, Somerset; ♿

As vast as it is magnificent, entering Southeast Asia's largest bookshop is a trek into literary jungle from which you might never emerge. One day they'll find a 40-year-old behind the Pets section who wandered in here when he was 12.

LOUIS VUITTON *Fashion*

☎ 6734 7760; 01-07, Ngee Ann City, 391 Orchard Rd; ☺ 10.30am-9pm; Ⓜ Orchard, Somerset; ♿

It's worth going at weekends just to see the queues of eager females and their anxious male companions waiting to get in. Join the queue, and look for a bag the replica hounds haven't copied yet.

BAG LADIES

Salivating handbag fetishists can send themselves to leather heaven on level 3 of the **DFS Galleria** and at **Paragon**: Louis Vuitton, Fendi, Gucci, Salvatore Ferragamo, Burberry, Dior, Prada, Coach, Valentino, YSL and Loewe! Bag yourself a bargain, or beat your credit card into submission. The less brand-conscious might try Far East Plaza, BHG at Parco Bugis Junction (Map pp68–9; 200 Victoria St) or hunt down knock-offs at Bugis St Market (p87).

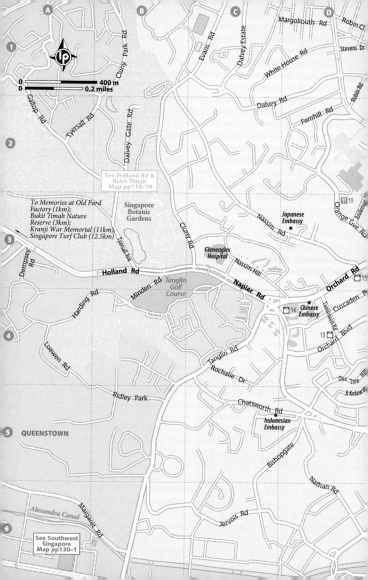

A1 B1 C1 D1

Margoliouth Rd
Robin Cl
Stevens Dr

Cluny Park Rd
Evans Rd
Dalvey Estate
White House Rd

Gallop Rd
Tyersall Rd
Dalvey Gate Rd
Dalvey Rd
Fernhill Rd
Robin Rd

0   400 m
0   0.2 miles

**See Holland Rd &
Bukit Timah
Map pp118–19**

Singapore
Botanic
Gardens

19
Orange Gve Rd
Japanese
Embassy
Nassim Rd

*To Memories at Old Ford
Factory (1km);
Bukit Timah Nature
Reserve (3km);
Kranji War Memorial (11km);
Singapore Turf Club (12.5km);*

Cluny Rd
Gleneagles
Hospital
Nassim Hill

Dempsey Rd
Holland Rd
Minden Rd
Napier Rd
Orchard Rd
15

Tyersall Ave
Tanglin
Golf
Course
14
Chinese
Embassy
Cuscaden Rd

Harding Rd
13
Orchard Blvd
Tomlinson Rd

Loewen Rd
One Tree
Tanglin Rd
Rochalie Dr
Jl Kelawar

Ridley Park
Chatsworth Rd
Indonesian
Embassy

QUEENSTOWN

Bishopgate
Nathan Rd

Alexandra Canal
Margaret Rd
Jervois Rd

**See Southwest
Singapore
Map pp130–1**

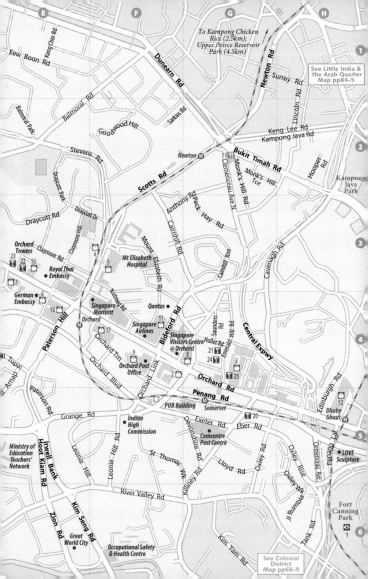

V

NEIGHBOURHOODS

ORCHARD ROAD

🏠 M)PHOSIS *Fashion*
☎ 6737 6539; B1-09/10, Ngee Ann City, 391 Orchard Rd; ⏰ 10.30am-9.30pm; Ⓜ Orchard, Somerset; ♿

M)phosis' Ngee Ann City branch (one of nine around town) stocks colour-coded miniature wisps of girly, slinky, sexy stuff; nice

ORCHARD MALL CRAWL
Singapore's shopping malls embody the prosperity and abundance so deeply craved by its citizens. The major malls open their doors around 10am and stay open until the last movie-goers and food court–feasters go home around midnight. The following are the major malls, heading roughly from east to west:

> **Tanglin Mall** (Map pp40-1; 163 Tanglin Rd) Expat haven (check the crowds of wives at Caffé Beviamo) with an excellent gourmet supermarket, shops for mothers and midrange boutiques.
> **Tanglin Shopping Centre** (Map pp40-1; 19 Tanglin Rd) The place for art, antiques and carpets. Try **Antiques of the Orient** (02-40) for maps, charts and photos, or the Asian academic titles at **Select Books** (03-15).
> **Wheelock Place** (Map pp40-1; 501 Orchard Rd) Apple devotees make pilgrimage to the mall's glass cone, which also houses a packed Borders and exclusive hair salons.
> **DFS Galleria Scottswalk** (Map pp40-1; 25 Scotts Rd) Souvenir hunting-ground and three levels of the usual expensive brand names in high fashion and perfume.
> **Wisma Atria** (Map pp40-1; 435 Orchard Rd) In-your-face frontage contains international high-street fashion, jewellery and electronics, and outstanding Food Republic food court.
> **Ngee Ann City** (Map pp40-1; 391 Orchard Rd) Chocolate blancmange–coloured doyen of Orchard, with Takashimaya department store (with fabulous basement food centre), the vast Kinokuniya bookshop, and resident gods Cartier, Chanel and Louis Vuitton.
> **Paragon** (Map pp40-1; 290 Orchard Rd) Classy, classy, classy: Givenchy, Ralph Lauren, YSL, Hugo Boss, Versace, Gucci, Jean-Paul Gaultier, Prada and people who love them. Great basement food selection.
> **Cathay Cineleisure Orchard** (Map pp40-1; 8 Grange Rd) Specialising in teen fashion, junk food, with a cinema and possibly the worst escalator layout on earth.
> **Centrepoint** (Map pp40-1; 176 Orchard Rd) Lively mall housing flagship old world Robinson's department store (great staff).
> **Plaza Singapura** (Map pp40-1; 68 Orchard Rd) Vast even by Orchard Rd standards and home to a 10-screen cinema, Carrefour supermarket, homeware, Barang Barang Asian furniture, fashion, food...everything!
> **The Cathay** (Map pp40-1; 2 Handy Rd) Streetwear, beauty and nail salons, 'lifestyle' shops and the excellent Picturehouse cinema behind an unfinished-looking Art Deco frontage.

KIDS 'R' US

Singapore's kids and teens are commercially catered for by a gaggle of clothes and toy shops. Here are some of the best places for kids and teens:

> **Bugis St Market** Two levels of cheap street clothes, bags, shoes and manicurists; see p87.
> **Far East Plaza** (Map pp40-1; 14 Scotts Rd) Teen mall most popular for cheap streetwear. Also hair and beauty salons, tattoo parlours, jewellery, electronics and secondhand books. Haggling possible.
> **Forum – The Shopping Mall** (Map pp40-1; 583 Orchard Rd; ⌚ 10am-10pm) Kid-sized DKNY, Ralph Lauren, Guess and Benetton gear.
> **Heeren** (Map pp40-1; 260 Orchard Rd) Hip, youth-orientated monolith, with massive multilevel HMV and warrens of local designer outlets on levels four and five.
> **Kinokuniya** (Map pp40–1) Kids' books by the truckload; see p39.
> **Mothercare** (Map pp68-9; ☎ 6513 3212; 02-03, Suntec City; ⌚ 11.30am-9pm) For all your bootie and mollycoddling requirements.
> **Robinsons** (Map pp40-1; ☎ 6733 0888; Centrepoint, 176 Orchard Rd; ⌚ 10.30am-10pm) A family-focused department store.
> **Toys 'R' Us** (Map pp40-1; ☎ 6235 4322; 03-03/25 Forum Shopping Mall, 583 Orchard Rd; ⌚ 10am-10pm) A celebration of international toydom.

knits; and elegant pieces by local designer Colin Koh. You'll increase your chances of actually fitting into something if you buy two pieces and sew them together.

🏠 PROJECTSHOP BLOOD BROTHERS *Fashion*
☎ 6735 0071; 03-41/44, Paragon, 290 Orchard Rd; ⌚ 10.30am-10pm; Ⓜ Orchard, Somerset; ♿
Popular local streetwear label selling summery gear (tank tops, cutesy t-shirts and sun dresses for girls; cargo pants for boys) plus bags, belts and wallets at reasonable prices, with unpretentious service. Can't decide what to buy? Refocus your desires over coffee and cake at the Projectshop Café next door. There's a branch in Wisma Atria Shopping Centre.

🏠 SUPERNATURE *Food*
☎ 6735 4338; 01-21, Park House, 21 Orchard Blvd; ⌚ 10am-7pm Mon, Tue, Thu & Sat, 10am-8pm Wed & Fri, 11am-6pm Sun; Ⓜ Orchard
Supernature is Singapore's best organic deli. Its shelves are heaving with chemical- and gluten-free veggies, groceries, baby food, wine and meats. It also does a roaring trade in organic coffee and take-away juices (try the predictably green 'Incredible Hulk').

TIED TO TRADITION

With new malls being shoehorned into every available space on Orchard Rd, why, many visitors ask, does the Thai Embassy occupy such large, prominent grounds in an area of staggeringly expensive real estate? Back in the '90s, the Thai government was reportedly offered $139 million for the site, but they turned it down. Why? Because selling the land, bought by Thailand for $9000 in 1893 by the revered King Chulalongkorn (Rama V), would be seen as an affront to his memory. And so, happily, it remains, drooled over by frustrated developers.

🎧 THAT CD SHOP *Music*
☎ 6238 6720; 01-01/02, Pacific Plaza, 9 Scotts Rd; 🕙 11am-midnight; Ⓜ Orchard

Filling a two-storey warehouse with stacks of CDs, comfy leather couches, subtle downlights, free coffee and a Nakamichi sound system that sets the chandeliers a-rockin', this feels less like consumerism and more like a party. Consider moving in on a permanent basis.

🍴 EAT

🍴 BOMBAY WOODLANDS
Indian, Vegetarian $$
☎ 6836 6961; B1-12, Tanglin Shopping Centre, 19 Tanglin Rd; 🕙 10.30am-3pm & 6-10pm; Ⓜ Orchard; 🧍 Ⓥ

Moved from its original location to a new spot a few doors down, this is still one of the hidden gems of the Orchard area. Try the bottomless lunchtime buffet or choose from the small but uniformly excellent menu of vegetarian staples.

🍴 DIN TAI FUNG *Taiwanese* $$
☎ 6836 8336; B1-03/06, Paragon Shopping Centre, 290 Orchard Rd; 🕙 11.30am-9.30pm Mon-Fri, 10am-10pm Sat & Sun; Ⓜ Orchard; 🦽

Taiwanese restaurant acknowledged even by hype-resistant luminaries such as Anthony Bourdain as producing the best dumplings on Earth (though some insist that only applies to the Taiwanese original). The signature dumplings *(xiao long bao)* are nevertheless sublime, the beef noodle soup rich and hearty, and the shrimp-pork wanton soup delectable. Be prepared to queue, especially at weekends, but the wait is worth it. A must.

🍴 FOOD REPUBLIC
Food Court $
Level 4, Wisma Atria Shopping Centre, 435 Orchard Rd; 🕙 11am-10.30pm; 🦽 🧍 Ⓥ

Perennially packed, it's survival of the quickest when it comes to grabbing a table at peak times, but the food is worth it. If it's full,

Michelle Chia
Actress, presenter, Mediacorp Studios

Favourite quiet, romantic spot? The Cliff (p101) restaurant at the Sentosa hotel. There's a separate area away from the main restaurant, which you can book. **The best view in Singapore?** The Singapore Flyer (p73). **Where would you eat on your last day in Singapore?** Breakfast at Ya Hua Rou Gu Cha on Keppel Rd (p133). They're only open for breakfast and lunch – and closed Mondays. Lunch at Kampong Chicken Rice (Map pp40–1) on Upper Thomson Rd – it's better than the other more well-known chicken rice places. Dinner would be at Newton Circus (p46), because they have everything there, but my favourites are the carrot cake and fish-ball noodles stalls. **Best place for after-dinner cocktails?** The Bar & Billiard Room (p76) at the Raffles Hotel. **Best green space to escape the crowds?** Upper Pierce Reservoir Park (Map pp40–1). It's so quiet and peaceful, and hardly anybody goes there.

head for the private sitting areas attached to the Chutneys Indian and Waan Waan Thai stalls, where you pay a little more. We also particularly like the teppanyaki counter and the beef noodles.

🍴 LUCKY PRATA Indian $
☎ 6235 5223; 01-42, Lucky Plaza, 304 Orchard Rd; ⏰ 11am-9pm; Ⓜ Orchard
One of those little surprises that pops up in unlikely and not entirely encouraging places. The north and south Indian fare is excellent, the fish-head curry particularly good. It's wildly busy at lunchtimes, so get there early, or expect to muck in with everyone else.

🍴 MARMALADE PANTRY
Café $$
☎ 6734 2700; B1-08, Palais Renaissance, 390 Orchard Rd; ⏰ 11.30am-9.30pm Mon-Fri, 10am-9.30pm Sat, 10am-4pm Sun; Ⓜ Orchard; ♿ 🚼 Ⓥ
Crisp white tablecloths, comfy booths and affluent ladies sizing each other up over the glossy mags set the scene at this sub-street café serving tasty morsels. The place to be seen on Sunday mornings, if you're not at a brunch (see boxed text, p77).

🍴 NEWTON CIRCUS
Hawker Centre $
Scotts Rd; ⏰ 5pm-4am; Ⓜ Newton; ♿ 🚼 Ⓥ

Vibrant and noisy, this famous hawker centre still has a great atmosphere. You could eat here for a year and never get bored. Well-known stalls include Boon Tat BBQ seafood, Hup Kee oyster omelette (stall 65) and, next to it, Singapore's most famous fishball noodles. Touts can be a problem for foreigners, but ignore them. The best stalls don't need to tout.

🍴 PROJECTSHOP CAFÉ
International $$
☎ 6735 6765; 02-20/21, Paragon Shopping Centre, 290 Orchard Rd; ⏰ 10am-8.30pm; Ⓜ Orchard; ♿ 🚼 Ⓥ
Sit out in the mall to watch Singapore's affluent sashay past, or sit inside the shop linked to the café for a more private setting. Sandwiches and pastas are reasonable, but the real reason to come here is the stupendous desserts. Banana Cream Pie tops our list, or try the key lime pie if you need a serious sugar hit. Sister restaurant PS Café (p124) at Dempsey Rd is a great spot for dinner.

🍴 SHANG PALACE
Chinese $$$
☎ 6213 4473; Ground, Shangri-La Hotel, 22 Orange Grove Rd; ⏰ 11.30am-2.30pm, 6.30-10.30pm Mon-Fri, from 1.30pm Sat & Sun; Ⓜ Orchard, then taxi; ♿
Among the best of the city's Chinese restaurants, Shang's sumptuous interior is matched

Singapore is a food paradise and there are plenty of tasty options to suit all budgets at Newton Circus

by its Cantonese food. Seafood is a particular speciality, along with classics such as Peking Duck, and there's a *dim sum* menu, if you want the atmosphere without the expense. Book in advance at weekends.

☂ DRINK
☂ DUBLINERS *Irish Pub*
☎ 6735 2200; 165 Penang Rd;
☺ 11.30am-1am Sun-Thu, till 2am Fri & Sat; Ⓜ Somerset
Lousy Irish pubs filled with bellowing, beer-bellied execs are omnipresent in Singapore, but this white colonial heritage building is a cut above the rest. Choose between the rough floorboards and cosy gloom inside, and nursing a Guinness and braving the traffic noise on the veranda.

☂ IPANEMA WORLD MUSIC BAR *Bar*
☎ 6738 3483; 02-43, Orchard Towers, 400 Orchard Rd; ☺ 7pm-5am Mon-Thu, 7pm-6am Fri & Sat, 1pm-4am Sun; Ⓜ Orchard
If it's sleaze you're after, look no further. This stalwart of Orchard

WORTH THE TRIP

The **Singapore Zoo and Night Safari** (☎ 6269 3411; www.zoo.com.sg, www.nightsafari .com.sg; 80 Mandai Lake Rd; zoo adult/child $16.50/8.50, zoo tram $5/2.50, Night Safari $22/11, Night Safari tram $10/5, combined zoo/Night Safari $30/15; ⏱ zoo 8.30am-6pm, night safari 7.30pm-midnight; Ⓜ Ang Mo Kio, then bus 138; ♿) are both world-class, with the zoo being constantly upgraded.

The zoo's showpiece animals include endangered white rhino, Bengal white tigers, polar bears, baboons and orang-utans. Wherever possible, moats replace bars, and the zoo is beautifully spread out over 28 hectares of lush greenery beside the Upper Seletar Reservoir.

Highlights are many – from the moment you step in to be greeted by free-ranging cotton-top tamarins and white-faced sakis and siamangs cavorting in the trees. The baboon enclosure, a large sandy area with cliffs, a waterfall and a stream fashioned to look like the Ethiopian hinterland, is worth the entrance fee alone.

Other primate areas also allow you to watch the likes of gibbons, the lively capuchins or proboscis monkeys, while the orang-utans, once marooned on a small island surrounded by gawping humans, have been cut loose and now get to hang around in the trees gawping down on the humans instead.

Another favourite is the Fragile Forest, a large netted dome where you'll have lemurs trotting across your path, flying foxes dangling by your head and hundreds of butterflies fluttering past your face.

Feeding times are staggered to allow you to catch most of them as you walk around, and the Zoo Management Tours (see Organised Tours, p194) are worth joining.

Some shows, such as those at the Elephants of Asia and polar-bear enclosures, may be a little circus-like for some – and there has been particular controversy surrounding the keeping of polar bears in a hot equatorial climate.

Next door, but completely separate from the zoo, is the acclaimed Night Safari. This 40-hectare forested park is home to 120 different species of animals, including tigers, lions and leopards. In the darkness the moats and other barriers seem to melt away and it actually looks like these creatures could walk over and take a bite out of you. The atmosphere is heightened even further by the herds of strolling antelope, which often pass within inches of the electric trams that take you around.

For an even creepier experience, walk through the enclosed Mangrove Walk, where bats flap around your head and dangle from trees a few feet above your head.

Both parks have plenty of decent food outlets and the zoo even boasts award-winning, clean and creatively designed 'outdoor' toilets!

If returning from the Night Safari by bus, you should aim to be on the bus by around 10.45pm to ensure you make the last train leaving Ang Mo Kio MRT at 11.28pm. A taxi to or from the city centre at that time costs around $20; there is a taxi stand outside, but the queues are often long and cabs can be maddeningly infrequent.

EMERALD HILL

A cobbled pedestrianised lane of crumbling, lantern-lit shophouses, there can be few more atmospheric spots in the city to stop for a drink – that is until you realise it's all a bit of a charade. That little neighbourhood bar strip is entirely owned by a single company, but even so, the drinking holes are all good, drawing crowds of locals and tourists alike.

The best are the Asian retro **No. 5** (☎ 6732 0818; ☽ noon-2am Mon-Thu, noon-3am Sat, 5pm-2am Sun), Mediterranean-style wine-and-tapas bar **Que Pasa** (☎ 6235 6626; ☽ 6pm-2am Sun-Thu, 6pm-3am Fri & Sat) and raucous rock pub **Ice Cold Beer** (☎ 6735 9929; ☽ 5pm-2am Sun-Thu, 5pm-3am Fri & Sat).

Rd's famous 'four floors of whores' is packed to the rafters with Western men and the girls hoping to collar them for the evening. However, it does have one of Singapore's best cover bands and, if you make it clear you're not interested, you'll soon be left alone.

A vibrant oddity – a skate park in Singapore!

☗ MUDDY MURPHY'S *Irish Pub*
☎ 6735 0400; Orchard Hotel Shopping Arcade; ☽ 11.30am-1am Mon-Thu, till 2am Fri & Sat, till midnight Sun

OK, OK, it's another Irish pub, but the substreet-level courtyard also singles this one out from the rest and makes it a perfect retreat from Orchard Rd. Live bands play here regularly – a few of the deedly-dee variety.

⭐ PLAY

⭐ NATIONAL YOUTH CENTRE SKATE PARK
☎ 6734 4233; Penang Rd; ☽ 7am-11pm; Ⓜ Somerset; ♿

One of Singapore's better at-tempts at embracing modern youth culture, the Skate Park is fully equipped with ramps and rails where boarders and bikers practise, pose and impress watch-ing members of the opposite sex. Occasionally, a temporary stage is set up for concerts.

>CHINATOWN & THE CBD

Just in time, Singapore realised Chinatown's narrow lanes of old shop-houses, with their shuttered windows and steep tiled roofs, were fit for more than tearing down. This old district, once home to opium dens, death houses, brothels and gang warfare, is still Singapore's most colourful.

Even within Chinatown there are distinct ethnic centres: Hokkien on Havelock Rd, Telok Ayer, China and Chulia Sts; Teochew on Circular Rd, Boat Quay and Upper South Bridge Rd; Cantonese on Lower South Bridge Rd, New Bridge Rd and Upper Cross St.

Pagoda, Temple and Trengganu Sts are the centre of the tatty tourist trade but have some decent antique shops. Market-weary visitors also head for the Sri Mariamman and Buddha Tooth Relic temples. Cross South Bridge Rd into a different world of top restaurants, hip bars, boutiques and trendy businesses packed into narrow Club St and Ann Siang Rd.

A stroll over Ann Siang Hill Park leads to Amoy and Telok Ayer Sts, a historical district of temples and shophouse eateries. Surrounding it all to the east and north are the looming skyscrapers of Singapore's financial district.

CHINATOWN & THE CBD

⊙ SEE
Buddha Tooth Relic
 Temple & Museum **1** E4
Chinatown Heritage
 Centre.....................**2** D3
Nam's Supplies..............**3** D3
Singapore General
 Hospital...................**4** B4
Speakers' Corner **5** E2
Sri Mariamman Temple..**6** E3
Thian Hock Keng Temple..**7** F4

🛍 SHOP
Eu Yan Sang...................**8** E4
Red Peach Gallery **9** D3
Wang San Yang **10** E3
Whatever......................**11** C4
Yue Hwa Chinese
 Products.................**12** D2
Zhen Lacquer Gallery ...**13** D3

🍴 EAT
Annalakshmi **14** F4
Blue Ginger..................**15** D5
Breeze.........................**16** E4
Broth **17** D5
Chiang Mai Palace........**18** F3
Erich's Wuerstelstand ..**19** D3
Hong Lim Complex.....(see 10)
Imbiss & Backstube......**20** D3
L'Angelus **21** E4
Lau Pa Sat Festival
 Market....................**22** G4
Maxwell Rd Hawker
 Centre.....................**23** E4
Ocean Curry Fish Head .**24** F4
Peach Garden **25** F2
Senso **26** E3
Smith St Hawker
 Centre.....................**27** D3
Ya Kun Kaya Toast &
 Coffee.....................**28** F3

Ⓨ DRINK
Backstage Bar **29** E3
Bar Sá Vanh **30** E4
Beaujolais Wine Bar.....**31** E4
Kazbar **32** F3
Le Carillon de l'Angleus**33** E4
Oosters **34** F3
Taboo...........................**35** D4
The Terrace ....(see 40)
The Toucan **36** D5
W Wine Bar **37** E3

▣ PLAY
Kenko Wellness Spa **38** E3
Line Dancing **39** F3
The Screening Room **40** E4
Urban Fairways **41** E3

Please see over for map

SEE

BUDDHA TOOTH RELIC TEMPLE & MUSEUM

☎ 6220 0220; www.btrts.org.sg; 288 South Bridge Rd; admission free; ☼ 7am-7pm; Ⓜ Chinatown; ♿

Impressive temple and museum constructed in 2007 primarily to house a Buddha Tooth Relic, which sits inside a 420kg solid-gold stupa in a dazzlingly ornate 4th-floor room. Get there at 10.30am or 7.30pm, when monks hold ceremonies to open the chamber. Also worth seeing are the peaceful rooftop garden, where a huge prayer wheel sits inside a 10,000 Buddha Pavilion, and the museum and the 100 Dragons Hall. Free vegetarian food in the basement.

CHINATOWN HERITAGE CENTRE

☎ 6325 2878; www.chinatownheritage.com.sg; 48 Pagoda St; adult/child $9.80/6.30; ☼ 9am-8pm; Ⓜ Chinatown; ♿

One of Singapore's less-trumpeted museums, this is one of our favourites: an evocative exploration of the grim, tough lives of early Chinese immigrants. Particularly effective are the recreations of the living conditions people in the area endured. There's a lot to take in, so keep your ticket stub and you can nip out for a breather and return later.

SRI MARIAMMAN TEMPLE

☎ 6223 4064; 244 South Bridge Rd; ☼ 6.30am-9pm; Ⓜ Chinatown; ♿

The colourful *gopuram* (entrance tower) of Singapore's oldest Hindu temple, built in its present form in 1843, with dozens of additions since, is one of the most photographed objects in the city. Sadly,

Sri Mariamman Temple in all its colourful glory

NEIGHBOURHOODS

CHINATOWN & THE CBD

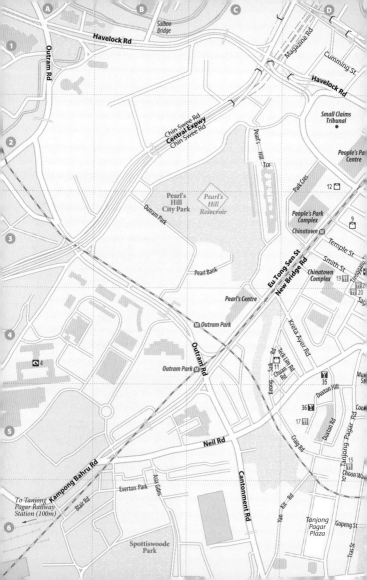

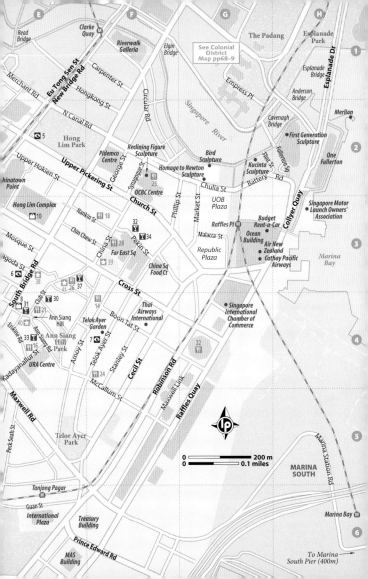

GETTING THERE & AROUND

> **MRT** – Raffles Place to Tanjong Pagar, or Clarke Quay to Chinatown take you from the CBD and quays area into Chinatown.
> **Bus** – 80, 145, 608 run the length of South Bridge Rd. In the other direction, 2, 12, 54 run up Eu Tong Sen St.

tourists crowd its magnificent door and its many shrines, outnumbering worshippers much of the time. Wait for a moment when there are no coach parties.

THIAN HOCK KENG TEMPLE

☎ 6423 4626; 158 Telok Ayer St; ☺ 7.30am-5.30pm; Ⓜ Chinatown, Tanjong Pagar, Raffles Place

Oddly, while Chinatown's most famous Hindu temple is swamped, its most famous Chinese temple is often a haven of tranquillity. It's

a beautiful, serene place, which was once a favourite landing point for Chinese sailors, before land reclamation pushed the sea far down the road.

🛍 SHOP

Though the main area of Chinatown has been swamped by stalls aimed at tourists (does anyone still buy those 'Fine City' T-shirts?), behind this wall of tattiness there are interesting antique, traditional-medicine and handicraft shops. Across South Bridge Rd, Club St has a few hip boutiques.

🏠 EU YAN SANG

Chinese Medicine

☎ 6223 5085; 269 South Bridge Rd; ☺ 9am-5.30pm Mon-Sat; Ⓜ Chinatown; ♿

Venerable Eu Yan Sang has enjoyed the fruits of official efforts to

FREEDOM OF SPEECH! (JUST DON'T MENTION FREEDOM OF SPEECH)

When Speakers' Corner (Map pp52–3) was established in Hong Lim Park in 2000, the ever spin-happy government and press hailed it as a step forward for Singaporean democracy and freedom of speech. Singaporeans love novelty, and in the first month 400 speakers addressed enthusiastic crowds. A year later only 11 braved the stand. Now, it's completely deserted and, cynics will say, a more accurate symbol of the state of free speech in a country that's politically apathetic anyway. In order to take your place at the soapbox, you have to be Singaporean, register in advance with local police, avoid blacklisted subjects such as religion, politics and ethnicity, and stay within Singapore's sedition laws. Still feel like speaking out?

REAPING THE PROFITS

Sharp-eyed wanderers will notice some curious objects on sale around Chinatown – miniature cars, houses, computers, mobile phones – all made of paper. They are offerings burned at funeral wakes to ensure the material needs of the dead are taken care of. Once, Sago Lane was home to so-called 'death houses', where people would place their dying relatives to spend their last days. This morbid practice was banned in 1961, but a few shops in the area, such as Nam's Supplies (Map pp52–3) on Smith St, still sell these paper objects.

propel traditional Chinese medicine back into the mainstream, with modern clinics and branches overseas. Consult a herbalist for $15, or get off-the-shelf remedies such as instant bird's nest (to tone the lung) or deer's tail pills (to invigorate the kidneys). Most remedies come with English instructions.

RED PEACH GALLERY
Homewares, Art

☎ 6222 2215; www.theredpeach.com; 68 Pagoda St; ☼ 11am-9pm Mon-Sat, noon-7.30pm Sun; Ⓜ Chinatown; ♿
One of the best bets if you're in the hunt for Ming-style home furnishings and Chinese artwork. There's no pretending the stuff is antique and the quality of the workmanship is good.

WANG SAN YANG *Teahouse*

☎ 6532 2707; www.wystm.com; Block 531, 01-61, Hong Lim Complex; ☼ 10am-9pm; Ⓜ Chinatown; ♿
Elegant specialty tea merchant whose location among the rough-and-ready bustle of the Hong Lim Complex gives it an injection of authenticity lacking in Chinatown's more tourist-friendly teahouses. Tea demonstrations on demand.

WHATEVER *Bookshop, Café*

☎ 6224 0300; www.whatever.com.sg; 20, 29A & 31 Keong Saik Rd; ☼ 9am-late; Ⓜ Chinatown; ♿
Singapore's middle-class affluence has fuelled a surging 'wellness' industry and Whatever is one of its principal players, offering classes in everything from yoga and meditation to the more esoteric healing disciplines. The bookshop glows with inspiration and there's an excellent vegetarian café. Some might find all that beatific harmoniousness to be, well, a little sickening.

YUE HWA CHINESE PRODUCTS *Department Store*

☎ 6538 4222; 70 Eu Tong Sen St; ☼ 11am-9pm; Ⓜ Chinatown; ♿
This five-storey department store stocks everything Chinese, from porcelain teapots and jade jewellery to slinky silk cheongsams, dried fish and medicinal herbs,

fungi and spices. Pick up some ginseng, a snakeskin drum or a jar full of seahorses for the road.

☐ ZHEN LACQUER GALLERY
Handicrafts

☎ 6222 2718; 1/1A/1B Trengganu St; ⏱ 9.30am-6.30pm; Ⓜ Chinatown; ♿

Generally kitsch but sometimes stylish, the shiny lacquered stuff at Zhen will at least keep your eyes entertained for a few minutes. Hand-painted jewellery boxes, placemat sets, utensils, plates and photo albums are the pick of the crop.

🍴 EAT

The absence of malls makes Chinatown one of Singapore's best eating districts, where sweaty hawker centres and cheap coffeeshops share pavement with world-class restaurants. Club St is the only exclusively upmarket area; everywhere else, the cheap and cheerful coexists happily with the rare and refined.

🍴 ANNALAKSHMI *Indian* $

☎ 6223 0809; www.annalakshmi .com.sg; 104 Amoy St; ⏱ 11am-3pm

Erich's Wuerstelstand offers sausages and sauerkraut in Chinatown. Odd? Yes, but people love it.

Mon-Sat; **M** Tanjong Pagar; &
& **V**

Something of an institution, this volunteer-run Indian vegetarian restaurant serves up excellent limitless lunchtime buffets that attract hordes of office workers. When you're finished just pay whatever you feel like to the cashier. From $5 to $10 is acceptable – it all goes to charity. Other branches at Lau Pa Sat and in Chinatown Point are open for dinner as well.

BLUE GINGER *Peranakan* $$
☎ 6222 3928; 97 Tanjong Pagar Rd; noon-2.30pm & 6.30-10.30pm; **M** Tanjong Pagar; & &

Fashionable, homely shophouse restaurant dishing up all the rich, spicy, sour Peranakan favourites, including the *ayam panggang* (grilled chicken in coconut and spices) that is the restaurant's claim to fame.

BREEZE *International* $$$
☎ 6511 3333; www.thescarlethotel .com; 31 Erskine Rd; 7pm-1am Mon-Sat; **M** Tanjong Pagar, Chinatown; & &

Slide into some designer togs and sashay up to the rooftop of the Scarlet Hotel with its impressive city views. Here the rich and fashionable dine on seafood feasts under the stars while keeping one eye on their phones.

BROTH *International* $$
☎ 6323 3353; www.broth.com.sg; 21 Duxton Hill; noon-2.30pm, 6.30-10.30pm Mon-Thu, noon-2.30pm, 7-11pm Fri, 7pm-11pm Sat; **M** Tanjong Pagar; & **V**

Set in a beautifully converted shophouse on a blissfully peaceful cobbled pedestrian street, Broth serves up excellent bistro classics (including a very good beef tenderloin). Proximity to dozens of sleazy karaoke bars hasn't diminished its atmosphere.

CHIANG MAI PALACE *Thai* $$
☎ 6538 2231; 01-27, China Square Central, 3 Pickering St; 11am-3pm, 6-10pm; **M** Raffles Place; & & **V**

Not much to look at, but Chiang Mai Palace takes our prize for the best Thai food in the neighbourhood (and the friendly staff). Try the fragrant, warming *om kai* (northern Thai chicken soup) or the *laap* (Lao–northeast Thai minced-meat salad).

ERICH'S WUERSTELSTAND *Austrian* $
☎ 9627 4882; Stall 2 & 3 Terrengganu St; 10am-8pm

An eccentric Austrian hawking very low-priced sausages and sauerkraut from a stall in Chinatown – it's hardly a surprise this place has achieved a certain fame. And deservedly so: what could be better than a hearty

NEIGHBOURHOODS

CHINATOWN & THE CBD

Choices. Decisions. The Maxwell Rd Hawker Centre has more than 50 stalls under one roof

sausage and beer (from across the lane) after a hot day in the city? Check out the German and Austrian breads and hearty Central European meals at his **Backstube** and **Imbiss** outlets opposite.

HONG LIM COMPLEX
Hawker Centre $

cnr South Bridge Rd & Upper Cross St; 🕑 **8am-10.30pm;** Ⓜ **Chinatown;** ♿
If you're sick of bumping elbows with tourists, head for this pocket of old-time Chinatown, where 'uncles' sit around watching the world go by and foreign faces still draw attention. The food centre is routinely crowded – try the famous Outram Park Fried Kway Teow (Block 531A, 02-18), or its rival, Cuppage (Block 536, 01-129). If the hawker centre

looks too full or intimidating, try Wuhan Food House (01-33).

L'ANGELUS *French* $$$
☎ **6225 6897; 85 Club St;** 🕑 **noon-2pm Mon-Fri, 7pm till late Mon-Sat;** Ⓜ **Chinatown;** ♿
A cosy and unstuffy French bistro famed for its *escargot* and chocolate cake. If it's a rainy night, tuck into the warming, incredibly filling *cassoulet* (bean stew with meat and sausage) washed down with a glass of something red and robust.

LAU PA SAT FESTIVAL MARKET *Hawker Centre* $
18 Raffles Quay; 🕑 **11am-3am;** Ⓜ **Raffles Place;** Ⓥ
Vying for the title of Most Famous Hawker Centre, this circular iron

structure dating back to 1894 even receives tour parties, who clamber from coaches and stand around looking uncomfortable. Singapore's 'upgrading' mania has bled some of the atmosphere from this venerable institution, but wandering its aisles and picking out your dinner is still a pleasure.

🍽 MAXWELL RD HAWKER CENTRE *Hawker Centre* $
cnr Maxwell Rd & South Bridge Rd;
🕒 **7am-10pm;** Ⓜ **Tanjong Pagar;**
♿ Ⓥ

If you want to get down and local in Chinatown, Maxwell Rd is it (along with Chinatown Complex). Sip soupy, sump oil–like coffee

with the 'uncles' in the morning, or battle the huge crowds at lunchtime. Stalls slip in and out of favour with Singapore's fickle diners so look for the queues to spot this week's fad. And who could pass up a bakery stall called Bread Pitt?

🍽 OCEAN CURRY FISH HEAD *Chinese* $
☎ **6324 9226; 181 Telok Ayer St;**
🕒 **11am-5pm;** Ⓜ **Tanjong Pagar;** ♿

Specialising in a Chinese version of the infamous South Indian dish, this street-corner eatery spills out onto the pavement at lunchtimes, when the plastic tables are full of office workers crowding around claypots and mopping their foreheads. If the

---

THE HAWKER CENTRE DECODED

It's not rocket science, but a visit to the hawker centre does require some insider knowledge.

> **First, find your table** Singaporeans always set up base camp before they go in search of food. And to do this, they use the humble packet of tissues. It confuses and confounds many newcomers, but to a Singaporean, a packet of tissues on a table or a seat is as good as erecting barbed wire and gun turrets – it means 'reserved'.

> **Second, find your food** Forget stall exclusivity – order as many things from as many stalls as you like, and ignore touts at places such as Newton Circus, East Coast Lagoon Food Village and Lau Pa Sat. It's actually illegal to tout.

> **Self-service, or delivery?** If a stall bears the sign 'self-service', that means you have to wait and carry the food to your table yourself. Other stalls ask where you're sitting and deliver food to you (which is why it's important to bag your table first).

> **Be seated and ye shall be found** Nearly all older hawker centres have roaming drinks staff, who will seek you out and take your order. At the more modern ones it's more usual to order from the drinks stalls.

> **Greasy hands?** Why do stalls never have tissues? Because most places are frequented by poverty-stricken tissue sellers, who'll come around selling five packets for a dollar. Help them out and buy some.

YOU AH, WHAT YOU EAT

A quick rundown of some classic Singapore dishes you're likely to encounter.

> **Ais Kacang** (Malay) Shaved ice covered with syrup, jelly, sweet corn and red beans.
> **Bak kut teh** (Hokkien) Pork-rib soup.
> **Bee hoon** (Hokkien) Thin rice-vermicelli noodles used in a variety of dishes.
> **Beef/chicken rendang** (Malay) Thick Malay-style curry.
> **Char kway teow** (Hokkien) Stir-fried noodles with cockles, Chinese sausage and egg in dark sauce.
> **Chicken rice** (Hainanese) Boiled chicken with stock-boiled rice and chilli-ginger dip.
> **Chilli crab** (Singaporean) Crab cooked with chilli, sweetish tomato sauce and egg.
> **Fish-head curry** (Indian) Single large fish head in spicy, rich, sour gravy, usually with tomato and okra.
> **Hokkien mee** (Hokkien) Yellow egg noodles stir-fried with prawns, pork and vegetables with an egg stirred in.
> **Katong laksa** (Malay) Rich, spicy coconut sauce with yellow or white noodles, prawns, cockles, fish cake, bean sprouts and laksa leaf.
> **Mee goreng** (Malay) Spicy fried noodles with tomato sauce, potato, cabbage and sometimes mutton.
> **Nasi lemak** (Malay) Coconut rice with fried fish and peanuts.
> **Oyster omelette** (Hokkien) Oysters fried with eggs, chives and tapioca flour.
> **Popiah** (Peranakan) Spring roll filled with vegetables and various meats or prawn.
> **Rojak** (Malay) Vegetable salad with chilli sauce, cucumber, fruit, onion and dough fritters.
> **Roti prata** (Indian) Fried flat bread (plain or with filling) served with curry sauce.
> **Sambal** (Malay) Condiment made from chilli, various spices and often shrimp paste, used to cook seafood, meat and vegetables.

fish head doesn't appeal, try the prawn-paste chicken, fried squid or chilli *kang kong* (water spinach).

🍴 PEACH GARDEN Chinese $$

☎ 6535 7833; Level 33, OCBC Centre, 65 Chulia St; ⏰ 11.30am-2.30pm & 6-10pm; Ⓜ Raffles Place; 🚻 Ⓥ

For a Chinese restaurant with a view, it's tough to beat this one. The food and service are immaculate too. Try to reserve a window table well in advance and tuck into

superb dim sum, or try the duck, roast goose or lobster noodles.

🍴 SENSO Italian $$$

☎ 6225 3534; 21 Club St; ⏰ noon-2.30pm & 6.30-10.30pm; Ⓜ Chinatown; 🚻 Ⓥ

There are hundreds of Italian restaurants in Singapore, but none can beat this restaurant in a former school for romantic atmosphere. Book a table in the courtyard under the stars for maximum effect (and hope it doesn't rain).

🍴 SMITH ST HAWKER CENTRE
Hawker Centre　　　$

Smith St; ⏰ **6pm till late;**
Ⓜ **Chinatown;** ♿
You can't quite beat dinner in the open air – and clearly thousands of people agree, which is why Smith St Hawker Centre is such a hit. Grab a table, order a barbecued seafood feast, an endless stream of cold Tigers, and your night is made.

🍴 YA KUN KAYA TOAST & COFFEE *Breakfast*　　$

☎ **6438 3638; 01-01, Far East Sq, 18 China St;** ⏰ **7.30am-7pm Mon-Fri, 9am-5pm Sat & Sun;** Ⓜ **Raffles Place;** ♿ 👶 Ⓥ
Though a chain of them is now spread across the island, none matches this for a sense of the original 1940s coffee, *kaya* (coconut jam) toast and runny-egg stall that spawned it. Grab a seat inside for a ringside view of the bustling, yelling, no-nonsense staff. Traditional Singapore breakfast at its cholesterol-laden, caffeine-charged, sugar-fuelled best.

🍸 DRINK

The shophouse renovation frenzy that has swept Chinatown has been a natural magnet for fashionable watering holes, which line Club

St and Ann Siang Rd. The Tanjong Pagar area has been a longstanding centre for the gay night-scene, while the larger bars around the Far East Sq area attract a mainstream office crowd intent on serious drinking.

🍸 BACKSTAGE BAR *Bar*
☎ **6227 1712; 13A Trengganu St;** ⏰ **7pm-2am;** Ⓜ **Chinatown;** ♿
The balcony at this cosy men's pub is a great spot to chat, flirt with local lads and otherwise play Rapunzel. Don't be put off by the 'PLU Members Only' sign downstairs – friends of the rainbow flag have automatic membership. The entrance is on Temple St.

🍸 BAR SÁ VANH *Bar*
☎ **6323 0145; 49 Club St;** ⏰ **3pm-2am Mon-Thu, 3pm-2am Fri & Sat;** Ⓜ **Chinatown**
Sá Vanh's soft candles shed light on dusky shadows as gorgeous svelte things flit by the fishpond and the water wall, expats sink into sunken lounges, platters of Asian tapas make the rounds, and ambient tunes snake into the night – all under the heavy-lidded gaze of Buddha himself.

🍸 BEAUJOLAIS WINE BAR *Wine Bar*
☎ **6224 2227; 1 Ann Siang Hill;** ⏰ **11am-midnight Mon-Thu, 11am-2am Fri, 6pm-2am Sat;** Ⓜ **Chinatown**

A tiny, raffish bar in a barely renovated shophouse, Beaujolais is the perfect antidote to the large corporate entertainment venues that are consuming the city. The upstairs lounge is a gem.

▼ KAZBAR *Pub*
☎ 6438 2975; 01-03, Capital Square Three; ⏲ 11.30am-midnight Mon-Fri, 5.30pm-midnight Sat; Ⓜ Raffles Place; ♿

Popular Middle Eastern–themed pub, with curtained nooks and deep sofas inside and bar tables outside. Male office workers seem strangely drawn to the place: surely nothing to do with the comely belly dancer doing the rounds in the early evening – must be the dips and pita bread.

▼ LE CARILLON DE L'ANGELUS *Wine Bar*
☎ 6423 0353; 24 Ann Siang Rd; ⏲ noon-midnight Mon-Fri, 6pm-midnight Sat; Ⓜ Chinatown; ♿

The excellent wines do justice to the superb tiled interior of this French wine bar. Lovely though it is upstairs, our favourite spot is the comfy chairs and sofa downstairs in a private little nook facing the chalkboard wine list. The cheese platter is a must.

▼ OOSTERS *Gastro-Pub*
☎ 6438 3210; 25 Church St; 01-04, Capital Square Three; ⏲ noon-midnight Mon-Fri, 5.30pm-midnight Sat; Ⓜ Raffles Place

All dark wood, brass and big windows, Oosters recreates the

TEA TIME
The very antithesis of the quick cuppa, traditional Chinese tea preparation is meant to impose a period of concentration, relaxation and reflection on the drinker.
> Warm pot and cups.
> Add tea to strainer in pot.
> Fill pot with hot water to rinse leaves, then pour out immediately into jug.
> Refill pot to brim.
> Drag lid across top of pot to remove bubbles, then place lid back.
> Pour hot water collected from rinsing process over the pot.
> Infuse for 60 seconds, then pour into jug to ensure even strength.
> Pour from jug to sniffing cups.
> Drinker pours tea from sniffing cup to drinking cup, then smells empty sniffing cup to evaluate aroma.
> Drink.
> Start process all over again, or lose patience and reach for tea bags.

Tan Boon Gee
Jazz drummer

How did you get your start? I was an architecture student at National University of Singapore when I joined the university jazz band. My first break came when Shawn Kelly was playing at Harry's Bar and they had no drummer for the night – someone recommended me to sit in. **Best places to see jazz in Singapore?** Apart from Jazz@Southbridge (p80), the Regent Hotel is good, Harry's Bar (Map pp68–9; Boat Quay) on Sunday nights is fantastic and BluJaz Café (p94) is good some nights. **Why is Singapore's live music scene so quiet?** The average Singaporean is not so interested – things like marriage, money and making a living take priority, so even people with talent often give up music because of other priorities. **Best acts you've played with?** Aaron Goldberg (pianist), Eugene Pao (guitarist) and Marcus Printup (trumpet).

cosy interior of a Belgian pub, with a wide range of beers (the Leffe Blonde on tap is a favourite) and hearty food. Try the Mussels.

☏ TABOO *Nightclub*
☎ 6225 6256; 65/67 Neil Rd; ☽ 8pm-2am Wed & Thu, 10pm-3am Fri, 10pm-4am Sat

Hottest gay dance club on the scene (for the moment, at least), always packed with the requisite line-up of shirtless gyrators, dance-happy straight women and regular saucy themed nights.

☏ THE TERRACE *Bar*
☎ 6221 1694; www.screeningroom .com.sg; Level 5, 12 Ann Siang Rd; ☽ 6pm-2am Mon-Thu, 6pm-3am Fri & Sat; Ⓜ Chinatown

The views across Chinatown and the CBD from this intimate rooftop bar, part of the hip Screening Room (opposite), are superb. Bag a comfy couch on the periphery, kick the shoes off and have a shouting-into-each-other's-ears conversation over the sound system.

☏ THE TOUCAN *Pub*
☎ 9467 0555; 15 Duxton Hill; ☽ 11am-1am Mon-Thu, 11am-2am Fri, 3pm-2am Sat; Ⓜ Tanjong Pagar; ♿

Unique among Singapore's Irish pubs in that it has a proper beer garden: a lawn, wooden benches, big umbrellas, even a wishing well.

☏ W WINE BAR *Wine Bar*
☎ 6223 3886; www.wwinebar.sg; 11 Club St; ☽ 5pm-1am; Ⓜ Chinatown; ♿

Tiny, intimate, relaxed, low-lit – everything you could want in a pre- or postdinner wine bar. There are low tables and sofas and, of course, a huge list of around 300 wines.

★ PLAY

★ KENKO WELLNESS SPA *Spa*
☎ 6223 0303; www.kenko.com.sg; 199 South Bridge Rd; reflexology per 30min $33, massages per 30min $49; ☽ 10am-10pm; Ⓜ Chinatown; ♿

Kenko is the McDonald's of Singapore's spas with branches throughout the city, but there's nothing drive-through about its foot reflexology, romantic couples' sessions ($328 per 2½-hour session) or Chinese and Swedish massage (Chinese is more forceful, using pointy elbows).

★ LINE DANCING *Dance*
www.cldas.com; Fire Gate, Far East Sq, 70 Telok Ayer St; ☽ 7-10.30pm Fri; Ⓜ Raffles Place

Every Friday evening at 7pm, like clockwork, up go the speakers, people arrive, on go the uniforms, the hats and the boots, and commuters driving along Cross St are treated to the arcane pleasures

Expect enchanting city views from the top of the Screening Room, Chinatown

of public line dancing. If the lure is too strong, saunter up to the desk in the corner and pay $3 to join in.

☆ THE SCREENING ROOM
Cinema
☎ 6221 1694; www.screeningroom .com.sg; 12 Ann Siang Rd; ⏱ noon-2.30pm & 6pm-late; Ⓜ Chinatown; ♿
All-in-one entertainment venue comprising two bars, screening room, bistro and function room. The highlights, in a city swamped by mainstream Hollywood, are the sofa-filled movie rooms and

the rooftop bar offering fantastic views across the district. Pay $55 for a Food & Film package.

☆ URBAN FAIRWAYS
Virtual Golf
☎ 6327 8045; www.urbanfairways.com; 27 Club St; off-peak/peak per group of 1-4 people $125/150; ⏱ 7am-1am Mon-Fri, 7am-5pm Sat & Sun; Ⓜ Chinatown; ♿ ♨
Billing itself as Asia's first virtual-golf centre, offering players a virtual round on the world's top courses – all in air-conditioned comfort. Popular with corporate groups.

>COLONIAL DISTRICT & THE QUAYS

If Little India and Chinatown are the soul of Singapore, then the Colonial District (Civic District) is its heart and the Quays are its fancy hairdo.

Home of its most photographed buildings and vistas, the Colonial District is an area of such architectural richness that a treasure seems to appear at every turn (see Walking Tour, p144). The list of heritage structures is endless: Raffles Hotel, City Hall, the Singapore Art Museum, the National Museum and Asian Civilisations Museum to name but a few. And increasingly, for a city that threatened to commit architectural suicide in the '60s and '70s, modern buildings such as the magnificent Esplanade are earning Singapore a cutting-edge reputation.

COLONIAL DISTRICT & THE QUAYS

🅞 SEE
Asian Civilisations
Museum **1** E6
at-Sunrise Global Chef
Academy..................(see 28)
Esplanade – Theatres
on the Bay **2** G5
Merlion............................ **3** F6
National Museum of
Singapore................. **4** D3
Peranakan Museum **5** D3
Singapore Art Museum .. **6** E2

🅐 SHOP
Funan – The IT Mall....... **7** E4
Mothercare.................... **8** G4
Robinsons...................... **9** F4
Royal Selangor **10** C5
The Cathay.................. **11** D2

🍴 EAT
Ah Teng's Bakery.......... **12** F3
Coriander Leaf............. **13** C5

Equinox......................... **14** F4
My Humble House ....(see 2)
No Signboard Seafood..(see 2)
Pierside Kitchen & Bar .. **15** F6
Royal China................. **16** F3

🍸 DRINK
Archipelago.................. **17** D6
Bar & Billiard Room...... **18** F3
Brewerkz..................... **19** C5
City Space ....(see 14)
Crazy Elephant **20** C5
Cuba Libre **21** C4
Harry's........................ **22** E6
New Asia Bar ....(see 14)
Paulaner Brauhaus...... **23** G4
Post Bar ....(see 15)
Rupee Room **24** C4

☆ PLAY
1 Nite Stand Comedy
Club **25** C5

Amrita Spa 26 F3
Attica............................ 27 C5
Black Box ....(see 28)
Drama Centre ....(see 28)
Esplanade – Theatres
on the Bay ....(see 2)
Fort Canning Centre..... 28 D3
G-Max Reserve Bungy.. 29 D5
Jazz@South Bridge...... 30 E5
Ministry of Sound........ 31 C5
Raffles Culinary
Academy.................. 32 F3
Singapore Dance
Theatre...................(see 28)
Singapore Repertory
Theatre................... 33 B4
The Arena 34 C5
The Arts House 35 E5
Theatreworks............(see 28)
Victoria Theatre &
Concert Hall............ 36 E5

Please see over for map

Down by the riverside is where much of Singapore has its fun: enough bars, microbreweries, restaurants and nightclubs are strung along the Quays to keep you occupied for a year.

SEE

ASIAN CIVILISATIONS MUSEUM

☎ 6332 2982; www.acm.org.sg; 1 Empress Place; adult/child $10/5; ⏰ 1pm-7pm Mon, 9am-7pm Tue-Thu, Sat & Sun, 9am-9pm Fri; Ⓜ Raffles Place; ♿

Housed in a magnificently restored 1865 building, the ACM is one of Singapore's icons and a must-see. Set over three levels, the 10 permanent exhibits explore traditional aspects of pan-Asian culture and civilisation, including all of Southeast Asia, China, India and Sri Lanka. The sheer scale of the museum is such that, for the uninitiated, the ACM Highlights guided tour (2pm Monday, 11am and 2pm Tuesday to Friday) is advisable – though they don't run from late December to early January.

ESPLANADE – THEATRES ON THE BAY

☎ 6828 8377; www.esplanade.com; 1 Esplanade Dr; guided tours adult/child $10/8; ⏰ 10am-6pm; Ⓜ City Hall; ♿

The design of Esplanade – Theatres on the Bay was the subject of much controversy when it was first built

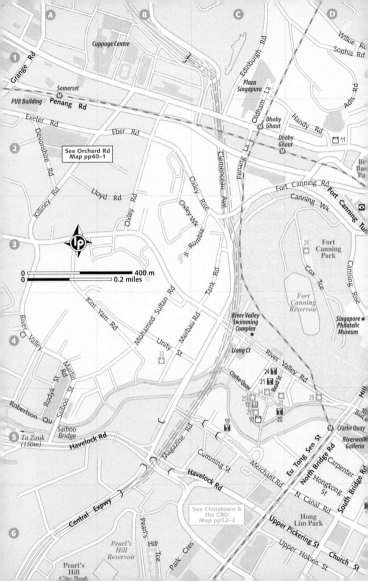

GETTING THERE & AROUND

> **MRT** – The North South Line from Dhoby Ghaut–City Hall–Raffles Place is the best means of traversing the area.
> **Bus** – 174 runs along Bras Basah Rd, then turns down North Bridge Rd to the river.

One of Southeast Asia's must stunning pieces of architecture, the Esplanade was created to announce Singapore's arrival on the world arts scene – and also as a challenge to the city's deep-seated conservatism. It succeeded on both counts, with a year-round program of opera, classical music, jazz, theatre, dance and a host of fringe events. Taking a guided tour – or a self-guided iTour using an electronic guide – is a great way of exploring this iconic structure. The website lists upcoming performances.

◉ NATIONAL MUSEUM OF SINGAPORE

☎ 6332 3659; www.nationalmuseum .sg; 93 Stamford Rd; adult/child $10/5; ☺ 10am-9pm; ♿

Imaginative, prodigiously stocked and brilliantly designed, the National Museum is good enough to deserve two visits. The Singapore History Gallery, which closes at 6pm, needs at least half a day (the free mobile electronic guide is a must, though ours froze halfway), and after 6pm, entry to the Living Galleries is free. The grand architecture alone makes it worth a visit.

◉ PERANAKAN MUSEUM

☎ 6332 7591; www.peranakanmuseum .sg; 39 Armenian St; adult/child $6/3; ☺ 9.30am-7pm, from 1pm Mon, till 9pm Fri; Ⓜ City Hall; ♿

Peranakan culture itself is dying out, but happily every aspect of

FLY EYES AND DURIANS

The Esplanade theatres, designed by a twin team of UK and local architects, cost a staggering $600 million and are built entirely on reclaimed land. The structure sits on a vast slab of rubber and, unusually, was constructed from the inside out. Not just visually impressive, the main Concert Hall inside is acoustically spectacular, containing a three-piece acoustic canopy and 84 computer-controlled doors and flaps hidden behind the hall's mahogany ribs that can make minute adjustments to the reverberations. The controversial exterior, variously compared to durians, fly eyes and honeycomb, is encased in aluminium shades set at various angles to maximise natural light while shielding the interior from the harsh sun. At night, it comes into its own, when interior lighting makes the whole building glow a beautiful green.

the colourful Straits Chinese, from clothing to customs to jewellery and food, is preserved in this sister institution of the Asian Civilisations Museum. Free admission from 7pm to 9pm on Fridays.

RAFFLES HOTEL
☎ 6337 1886; www.raffleshotel.com; 1 Beach Rd; Ⓜ City Hall; ♿

Whatever ostentatious modern projects Singapore undertakes now or in the future, Raffles Hotel will likely always be its most famous landmark. There's just something about the sight of that snow-white façade, the brushed-gravel drive, the Sikh doorman, the whispers of history. Astonishing to think it was scheduled for demolition in 1987, before a $160 million facelift restored it to glory.

SINGAPORE ART MUSEUM
☎ 6332 3222; www.nhb.gov.sg/SAM; 71 Bras Basah Rd; adult/child $8/4, noon-2pm Mon-Fri & 6-9pm Fri free admission; ⏱ 10am-7pm Mon-Thu, Sat & Sun, 10am-9pm Fri; Ⓜ Dhoby Ghaut, City Hall; ♿

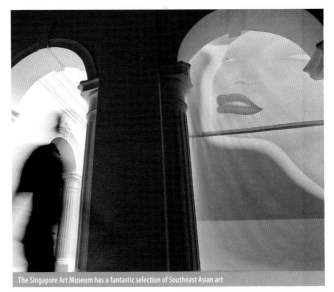
The Singapore Art Museum has a fantastic selection of Southeast Asian art

Dr Kenson Kwok
Director, Asian Civilisations Museum (p67)

Favourite exhibits? The Dehua porcelain collection. They were donated from a local collector and I invested a lot of energy and emotion in persuading her to donate them. **Best time to visit?** Avoid afternoons in May and November, when most of the school parties come! **Exhibit that was hardest to acquire?** The Chola bronze of Shiva, Parvati and Skanda. There was a mix-up and we missed the bid by an hour when it first came up for auction in New York. Luckily, the buyer put it up for sale again two years later. **The museum's best-kept secret?** A small 5th-century figure of Buddha about 20cm tall. It's very important as it's one of the earliest to be found in Southeast Asia, but it's often overlooked by visitors. **Top tip for visitors?** Go to see the golden textiles in Gallery 4a – it's the only gallery anywhere proposing a link between jewellery and textiles in Southeast Asian culture.

Magnificently restored, the Singapore Art Museum houses one of the finest collections of Southeast Asian art, both traditional and contemporary, and also hosts frequent travelling exhibitions. Major local artists such as Lim Tze Peng and Chen Chong Swee are also represented.

SINGAPORE FLYER
☎ 6333 3311; www.singaporeflyer.com.sg; Raffles Ave; adult/child $29.50/20.65; ⏰ 8.30am-10.30pm; Ⓜ City Hall; ♿

This is the world's largest observation wheel (beating the London Eye by 30m) and one of the key Marina Bay developments. The 30-minute ride is best done on a clear blue day, or on a clear night, when the lights of Indonesia and Malaysia frame the spectacular pan-Singapore views. Until future river-taxi services (2008), a pedestrian bridge (2009) and the MRT Circle Line (2010) are in place, the best way to get there is the shuttle service from City Hall MRT station (10am to 8pm daily, every 30 minutes; adult/child $2/1).

SHOP

FUNAN DIGITALIFE MALL *IT*
☎ 6336 8327; www.funan.com.sg; 109 North Bridge Rd; ⏰ 10.30am-9.30pm; Ⓜ City Hall; ♿

Tech mall of choice for people who prefer to pay a bit more for branded products and cast-iron guarantees, rather than brave the aisles of Sim Lim Square (p89). **Challenger Superstore** (☎ 6339 9008;

STREET SCULPTURE

Singapore is dappled with a healthy crop of public sculpture by acclaimed local and international artists. Check these out:

> **Abundance** (Map pp68–9) by Sun Yu Li – Suntec City
> **Between Sea & Sky** (Map pp68–9) by Olivier Strehelle – Marina Mandarin Hotel, 6 Raffles Blvd
> **Bird** (Map pp52–3) by Fernando Botero – UOB Plaza, Boat Quay
> **Homage to Newton** (Map pp52–3) by Salvador Dali – UOB Plaza, Boat Quay
> **LOVE** (Map pp40–1) by Robert Indiana – Penang Rd
> **Millennium** (Map pp68–9) by Victor Tan – Empress Place
> **Reclining Figures** (Map pp52–3) by Henry Moore – OCBC Centre
> **Seed sculptures** (Map pp68–9) by Singaporean artist Han Sai Por – Esplanade waterfront garden
> **Six Brushstrokes** (Map pp68–9) by Roy Lichtenstein – Millenia Walk, 9 Raffles Blvd
> **First Generation** (Map pp52–3) by Chong Fat Cheong – Cavenagh Bridge

Level 6) is the best one-stop shop for all IT needs.

ROYAL SELANGOR *Crafts*

☎ 6268 9600; 01-01 Clarke Quay;
🕙 9am-9pm; Ⓜ Clarke Quay

If Uncle Jim has always craved his own personalised tankard, here's your chance to get it for him. Indulge the short pewter-smithery demonstration, then admire the range of other articles, from jewellery to hip flasks, Malaysia's pewter specialists turn out.

🍴 EAT

🍴 AH TENGS BAKERY

Café $$

☎ 6412 1816; Raffles Hotel Complex, 1 Beach Rd; 🕙 7.30am-5.30pm;
Ⓜ City Hall; ♿

Perfect spot for a coffee-and-pastry breakfast, evoking a more genteel age with its marble-topped tables and clinking china. The dim sum makes a pretty decent afternoon snack, too.

🍴 CORIANDER LEAF

Asian Fusion $$

☎ 6732 3354; www.corianderleaf.com; 02-03, 3A Merchant Court, River Valley Rd; 🕙 noon-2pm & 6.30-10pm Mon-Fri, 6.30-10.30pm Sat; Ⓜ Clarke Quay; ♿ Ⓥ

An exercise in fusing the tiny morsels and artistic sauce (or should we say jus?) dribbles of nouvelle cuisine with traditional Asian flavours. Largely, it works, though the menu can be a little disorienting (hmm...Scottish salmon, miso cod or Thai barramundi?). Also runs highly regarded cooking courses.

🍴 EQUINOX *International* $$$

☎ 6837 3322; Level 70, Swissôtel, The Stamford, 2 Stamford Rd; 🕙 noon-2.30pm & 7-11pm;
Ⓜ City Hall; ♿ Ⓥ

If it wasn't for the incredible views, this might be rated an average restaurant. As it is, 70 floors up you won't care that the food is good, but not great. Book ahead, ask for a windowside table and chances are you'll spend so much time looking outside you'll forget to eat anyway. After dinner, head to City Space (p76) to continue gawping.

TEH WHAT?

Forget your lattes, mochas and macchiatos. Before taking on a Singapore-style coffeeshop, you need to learn a whole different lingo.

> **kopi** – coffee with condensed milk
> **teh** – tea with condensed milk
> **kopi-o/teh-o** – black coffee/tea with sugar
> **kopi-c/teh-c** – coffee/tea with evaporated milk and sugar
> **kopi-peng/teh-peng** – iced coffee/tea
> **teh tarik** – literally 'pulled tea', a sweet spiced Indian tea

🍴 LEI GARDEN *Chinese* $$$
☎ 6339 3822; 01-24, CHIJMES, 30 Victoria St; ⏱ 11.30am-3pm, 6-9.30pm; Ⓜ City Hall; ♿

Firm favourite for fancy Chinese dinners, the seafood at Lei is particularly well done (try the cod), but the roast pork also attracts a loyal following. Service can be patchy, so avoid when extremely crowded.

🍴 MY HUMBLE HOUSE *Chinese* $$$
☎ 6423 1881; www.tunglok.com; 02-27, Esplanade Mall, 8 Raffles Ave; ⏱ 11.45am-3pm & 6.30-11pm; Ⓜ City Hall; ♿

We're not sure if the name is ironic, but humble is not the first word that comes to mind when you clap eyes on the outlandish décor (designed by Chinese artist Zhang Jin Jie) and contemplate set lunches with names such as 'The Wind Wafts Above the Shoulder' and 'Memories of that Spring'. A memorable experience.

🍴 PIERSIDE KITCHEN & BAR *Fusion Seafood* $$$
☎ 6438 0400; 01-01, One Fullerton, 1 Fullerton Rd; ⏱ noon-3pm & 6-10pm; Ⓜ Raffles Place; ♿

Pierside's minimalist alfresco stylings earn the Singapore stamp of cool. Mirrored walls double the area the waiters need to cover – they glide around distributing plates of snapper pie, cumin-spiced crab cakes and lobster gumbo to well-heeled diners.

🍴 ROYAL CHINA *Chinese* $$$
☎ 6338 3363; 03-09, Raffles Hotel, 1 Beach Rd, ⏱ noon-3pm, 6-10.30pm; Ⓜ City Hall; ♿ Ⓥ

An excellent spot for afternoon dim sum, though you'll likely need to reserve a table. Have a light breakfast and fill up on scallop dumplings, crispy duck and lobster noodles.

🍴 TIFFIN ROOM *Indian* $$$
☎ 6431 6156; Lobby, Raffles Hotel, 1 Beach Rd; ⏱ 7am-7pm; Ⓜ City Hall; ♿ Ⓥ

The very name evokes pith helmets, linen suits and parasols, and the elegant interior only reinforces the image. Open all day, but best visited for the dinner buffet starting at 7pm, which is something close to curry heaven, though you may need to be carried out after.

🍸 DRINK

🍸 ARCHIPELAGO *Microbrewery*
☎ 6327 8408; www.archipelagobrewery.com; 79 Circular Rd; ⏱ 3pm-1am Mon-Thu & Sun, 4pm-3am Fri & Sat; Ⓜ Raffles Place; ♿

Hopping merrily on the Singapore microbrewery bandwagon, Archipelago has embarked on an aggressive campaign to sell its Asian-accented beers in other bars across the island, but this, its flagship pub on a Y-junction in mildly seedy Circular Rd, is still the best place to enjoy them.

Y BAR & BILLIARD ROOM *Bar*
☎ 6412 1816; www.raffleshotel.com; 1 Beach Rd; ⏱ 11.30am-10pm; Ⓜ City Hall; ♿
Forget the Long Bar, this is the quintessential Raffles drinking hole. Gentle lighting, genteel service, the clack of billiard balls, and a breezy veranda next to the spot where Somerset Maugham used to set up his typewriter.

Y BREWERKZ *Microbrewery*
☎ 6438 7438; 01-05, Riverside Point Centre, 30 Merchant Rd; ⏱ noon-midnight Sun-Thu, noon-1am Fri & Sat; Ⓜ Clarke Quay; ♿
The first among Singapore's crop of microbreweries and still among the best – and certainly the biggest. Some might prefer the more intimate surroundings of its rivals, but Brewerkz manages to combine large scale with great service – something of a rarity in Singapore. The beers are uniformly superb, and lunchtime boozers

will find the $4.99 pints from noon to 3pm an invitation to dispense with other plans for the day.

Y CITY SPACE *Lounge Bar*
☎ 6837 3322; Level 70, Swissôtel, The Stamford Singapore, 2 Stamford Rd; ⏱ 5pm-1am; Ⓜ City Hall; ♿
Deep armchairs, light jazz, Cuban cigars, fortified wines and stunning nighttime views over the island – this is the kind of place that makes you wish you owned a velvet smoking jacket.

Y CUBA LIBRE *Bar*
☎ 6338 8982; Block B, 01-13, Clarke Quay; ⏱ 6pm-1am Sun-Thu, 6pm-3am Fri & Sat; Ⓜ Clarke Quay; ♿
Follow the sound of trilling trumpet for a night of mojitos,

THE PADDLE POP LION

Just what is that thing endlessly spouting water into Marina Bay? Half-lion, half-fish, it's tempting to assume the **Merlion** (Map pp52-3) is some mythical creature steeped in Malay or Chinese mythology. In fact, it's a mythical creature steeped in the imagination of a Mr Fraser Brunner, who designed it for the Singapore Tourism Board in 1964 when the board decided the city needed an iconic emblem. At the Singapore International Comedy Festival in 2006, an Irish comedian somewhat cruelly noted its similarity to the logo that adorns Australia's Paddle Pop ice cream.

live Cuban music and dancing, or alternatively sit at a table, get drunk and watch parades of eager Singaporean salsa students going through the motions. Raucous and fun.

HARRY'S BAR *Pub*
☎ 6538 3029; 28 Boat Quay; ⏲ 11am-1am Sun-Thu, 11am-2am Fri & Sat; Ⓜ Raffles Place; ♿

The original and best. Harry's is a classic financial-district hang-out that gained moderate infamy as the haunt of Barings-buster Nick Leeson and remains a favourite for its jovial atmosphere and great live jazz, blues and R&B.

NEW ASIA BAR *Bar*
☎ 6831 5681; Level 71-72, Swissôtel, The Stamford Singapore, 2 Stamford Rd; ⏲ 3pm-late; Ⓜ City Hall; ♿

Singapore's most spectacular views join forces with a giant curvilinear mother-of-pearl wall, soaring ceilings and a VIP mezzanine for a drinking experience management insists will leave you feeling 'charged' (as opposed to 'overcharged', hopefully). There's a $25 cover charge at weekends.

PAULANER BRAUHAUS *Microbrewery*
☎ 6883 2572; www.paulaner.com.sg; 01-01, Times Square, Millenia Walk, 9

> ## JUST ANOTHER SOZZLED SUNDAY
>
> Singaporeans have enthusiastically embraced the British penchant for the Sunday champagne brunch, to the extent that most major hotels lay them on, typically kicking off at noon and frequently offering free-flow champagne. It's a competitive market, so checking local papers and what's-on magazines such as *I-S* or *Time Out* will often turn up deals. Popular haunts include **Town** (☎ 6877 8128) at the Fullerton Hotel, **mezza9** (☎ 6416 7189) at the Grand Hyatt, **Oscar's** (☎ 6334 8888), inside the Conrad Centennial, **Equinox** (☎ 6837 3322), 70 floors above Singapore at Swissôtel, The Stamford Singapore, or the **Bar & Billiard Room** (☎ 6412 1816) at Raffles.

Raffles Blvd; ⏲ 11.30am-1am Sun-Thu, till 2am Fri & Sat; Ⓜ City Hall

Wear your best pastel-striped shirt or power dress to mix with the business crowd downing highly addictive German beers at this convention-centre microbrewery. The inconvenient location at soulless Suntec City means that once you've made the effort to get here, you might as well dig in for the long haul. Two more please, fraulein.

POST BAR *Bar*
☎ 6733 8388; Fullerton Hotel, 1 Fullerton Rd; ⏲ noon-2am; Ⓜ Raffles Place; ♿

COLONIAL DISTRICT & THE QUAYS

Retaining the original post-office ceiling, decked out with modern sculptures and some decidedly futuristic underfloor lighting, Post Bar exudes class without snobbery and mixes an outstanding mojito. Worth dressing up for.

▼ RUPEE ROOM *Bar*

☎ 6334 2455; www.harrys.com.sg /Rupee.htm; 01-15, The Foundry, Clarke Quay; ⏰ 5pm-4am; M Clarke Quay; ♿

You've been practising those shoulder shakes in your bedroom for months, now it's time to don the nylon shirt, do up a couple of buttons, stick on the fake moustache and get to it yah? For a night of pure fun and silliness,

the Bollywood beats here are hard to top. A $15 cover charge applies Friday and Saturday.

★ PLAY

★ 1 NITE STAND COMEDY CLUB *Comedy*

☎ 6334 1954; www.the1nitestand.com; Block A, 01-04, Clarke Quay, 3 River Valley Rd; tickets $50; ⏰ noon-2am; M Clarke Quay; ♿

There are belly laughs aplenty at this big, carpeted bar, with mostly overseas stand-ups hamming it up for an appreciatively drunk crowd. An energetic house band keeps the masses entertained in-between acts.

★ AMRITA SPA *Spa*

☎ 6336 4477; www.amritaspa.com; 06-01, Raffles The Plaza, 60 Bras Basah Rd; foot and back massage $85, facials $85-320, body massage $150-175, waxing $20-95; ⏰ 10am-9pm, pool & gym 24hr; M City Hall; ♿

Top-of-the-range spa featuring a 24-hour pool and gym, plus all the requisite scrubs, waxings, massages and physical refurbishments. As you'd expect from anything bearing the Raffles name, it's all class.

★ ATTICA *Nightclub*

☎ 6333 9973; www.attica.com.sg; 01-12, Clarke Quay; ⏰ 5pm-3am Sun-Tue &

THE SINGAPORE SLING

It's a mystery to us why anyone would drink cough syrup for enjoyment, but evidently many people love this famous cocktail, invented at Raffles Hotel by barman Ngiam Tong Boon, so here's the recipe:

> 30mL gin
> 15mL cherry brandy
> 120mL pineapple juice (or soda)
> 15mL lime juice
> 10mL Cointreau
> 10mL Benedictine herbal liqueur
> 15mL Angostura bitters

Shake with ice, decant into highball glass, then decorate with cherry. Err...yum?

BEER TODAY, GONE TOMORROW .

If you find yourself wandering around cursing because some bar or restaurant we said was superb has vanished into thin air, bear in mind that Singapore's night scene is notoriously erratic. The law in Singapore gives minimal protection to tenants, and often the demise of a bar will be the result of a dispute with the landlord, rather than its unpopularity.

Thu, till 4am Wed, Fri & Sat;
Ⓜ **Clarke Quay**

Attica has secured a loyal following among Singapore's notoriously fickle clubbers, modelling itself on New York's hippest clubs but losing the attitude somewhere over the Pacific. The outdoor section is mostly colonised by 30-something expats, who find all the noisy dancing kids inside a bit too much. A \$25 cover charge includes two drinks.

⭐ CRAZY ELEPHANT *Blues Bar*

☎ 6337 7859; www.crazyelephant.com; 01-03, Clarke Quay; Ⓧ 5pm-2am Sun-Thu, till 3am Fri & Sat; Ⓜ Clarke Quay; ♿
If the remodelled Clarke Quay is a collection of eager-faced college kids, then Crazy Elephant is the crusty bloke in the corner watching them out of the corner of his eye and shaking his head. One of

Singapore's oldest, trustiest live-music venues, this is the place to ditch all that electronic nonsense and listen to some serious, loud rock and blues.

⭐ ESPLANADE – THEATRES ON THE BAY *Theatre*

☎ 6828 8377; www.esplanade.com; 1 Esplanade Dr; guided tours adult/child \$10/8; Ⓧ 10am-6pm; Ⓜ City Hall; ♿
Where to begin? In the outstanding Concert Hall, the world-class theatre, the host of smaller performance spaces? The Esplanade roused Singapore from its artistic coma and placed it firmly at the centre of the Asian arts world. There are more than a thousand performances in here every year, so there's no excuse for missing a chance to visit.

⭐ G-MAX REVERSE BUNGY *Thrill Ride*

☎ 6338 1146; Clarke Quay; per ride \$40; Ⓧ 1pm-1am Mon-Thu & Sun, 1pm-2am Fri & Sat; Ⓜ Clarke Quay
Flying upwards into the air at 200km/h inside a plastic pod attached to some elastic bands? Something tells us this is a Kiwi invention. A few Clarke Quay beers might improve your courage to have a go, but your stomach might not agree. Less terrifying is the neighbouring giant swing.

DRAMA QUEENS

Singapore's more dynamic and contemporary theatre groups produce both edgy and more accessible works at various venues around town. They often struggle for audiences and funds, but their undoubted passion keeps them alive. Banners advertising shows are usually plastered around town, or check listings in local magazines and newspapers. Groups include **Theatreworks** (www.theatreworks.org.sg), **The Theatre Practice** (www.ttp.org.sg), Singapore's sexiest and often most daring company, **Wild Rice** (www.wildrice.com.sg) and cutting-edge improvisational group **Cake** (www.caketheatre.com).

✪ GUINNESS THEATRE Theatre

☎ 6337 7535; www.substation.org; 45 Armenian St; ◷ box office noon-8.30pm Mon-Fri & 2hr before shows; Ⓜ City Hall
Part of the Substation experimental-arts complex, this small theatre (painted Irish stout black) promotes works by emerging local artists. Many shows are free, some have ticket prices. There are also regular workshops for poetry, painting and suchlike.

✪ JAZZ@SOUTHBRIDGE

Jazz Bar
☎ 6327 4671; www.southbridgejazz .com.sg; 62b Boat Quay; ◷ 5.30pm-1am Mon-Thu, 5.30pm-2am Fri & Sat; Ⓜ Clarke Quay, Raffles Place

It's not easy to find top nonclassical musical acts in Singapore, but this relaxed bar has come up trumps. Run by an irrepressible vibe-playing enthusiast, it regularly features performers from around the world, but it's worth going most nights to see the house band, especially magnificent but largely unheralded drummer Tan Boon Gee (see p63). Regular bassist Eddie Jansen and occasional pianist Mario Sero are also excellent.

✪ MINISTRY OF SOUND

Nightclub
☎ 6333 9368; www.ministryofsound .com.sg; Block C, 01-07, Clarke Quay; men $15-25, women free-$20; ◷ 9pm-3am Wed-Sat; Ⓜ Clarke Quay; ♿
When those decadent Brits came swaggering into town to pose a challenge to all-conquering Zouk, a few thought it wouldn't last. Wrong. MoS can now arguably claim to be the city's top club, and the enormous queues back it up. Seven rooms, superb digital sound and light, a chequered dance floor and a 20ft water curtain, not to mention hordes of the nation's youth. Women get in free on Wednesday.

✪ SINGAPORE REPERTORY THEATRE Theatre

☎ 6733 8166; www.srt.com.sg; DBS Arts Centre, 20 Merbau Rd; tickets $30-80; 🚌 33, 54, 139, 195

At the bigwig of the Singapore theatre scene, expect to see repertory standards such as *Death of a Salesman* and *The Glass Menagerie*, as well as modern local works.

⭐ SINGAPORE SYMPHONY ORCHESTRA *Classical Music*

☎ 6348 5555; www.sso.org.sg; Esplanade Theatre, 1 Esplanade Dr; Ⓜ Raffles Place

The outstanding SSO likes its venues grand – it plays regularly at its Esplanade home and also at the splendid Victoria Concert Hall (Map pp68–9). Its most memorable of performances is on the Symphony Stage in the Singapore Botanic Gardens (p117).

⭐ THE ARENA *Live music*

☎ 6338 3158; www.thearenalive.com.sg; 01-08, 3B Clarke Quay; ⏰ 5pm-4am Tue-Thu, 5pm-5am Fri-Sun; Ⓜ Clarke Quay; ♿

Touted as the largest live-music space in Singapore, this slick venue wheels out international bands and DJs for short residences or one-off gigs. Expect danceable mainstream Top 40, hip-hop and house to a cashed-up crowd.

⭐ ZOUK *Nightclub*

☎ 6738 2988; www.zoukclub.com.sg; 17 Jiak Kim St; entry $20-35; ⏰ Zouk & Phuture 8pm-3.30am Wed, Fri & Sat, Wine Bar 6pm-3.30am Mon-Sun; 🚕 taxi

Ibiza-inspired Zouk is a regular destination for globe-trotting DJs. Five bars, 2000-capacity, roomy dance floor – there's guaranteed bar access and plenty of space to cut the rug. Minimum-age entry is 21 for women, 23 for men.

Clarke Quay is home to bars, nightclubs, restaurants and a comedy club

>LITTLE INDIA & THE ARAB QUARTER

The closest you'll get to seeing what old Singapore city was like, Little India is a ramshackle, colourful, disorderly sort of place, where life tumbles along with an unfettered liveliness largely lost from the rest of the city. Goods crowd the five-foot ways, bhangra thuds from speakers, shopkeepers still paint signs on concrete pillars, irresistible food smells waft into the street and men clad in *dhoti* (loincloth) lounge around the market gossiping. It's like India with all the confronting bits taken out.

The quieter Arab Quarter, dominated by the large Sultan Mosque, has developed a low-key scene of its own, assisted by the pedestrianisation of Bussorah St. A clutch of Middle Eastern eateries and new shops has revitalised the area – and at night the fragrant smoke of *shisha* (flavoured

LITTLE INDIA & THE ARAB QUARTER

👁 SEE
Kuan Im Thong Hood
  Cho Temple................... 1 C7
Sri Srinivasa Perumal
  Temple.......................... 2 D3
Sri Veeramakaliamman
  Temple.......................... 3 C5
Sultan Mosque 4 E6
The Gateway.................... 5 E7

🛍 SHOP
Bugis St Market................ 6 C7
Curiocity Gallery............. 7 B7
Edge................................. 8 C7
Golden Mile Complex .. (see 31)
Grandfather's Collections 9 E7
Haji Lane Shops............. 10 D7
Indian Classical Music
  Centre......................... 11 B6
Indian Handicraft
  Centre......................... 12 C6

Khan Mohamed Bhoy
  & Sons 13 C5
Little Shophouse.......... (see 8)
Melor's Curios............... 14 E7
Mustafa Centre.............. 15 C4
Sim Lim Sq.................... 16 C6
Sungei Rd Thieves
  Market....................... 17 D6
Tekka Centre.............. (see 35)

🍽 EAT
Al-Tazzag...................... 18 E7
Ananda Bhavan............ 19 B6
Ananda Bhavan............ 20 B5
Ananda Bhavan............ 21 B6
Ananda Bhavan............ 22 D4
Andhra Curry................ 23 B5
Anjappar...................... 24 C4
Banana Leaf Apolo 25 B5
Café Le Caire................ 26 E7
Chettinadu.................... 27 B5

French Stall 28 D3
Gayatri......................... 29 B4
Ghandi......................... 30 B5
Golden Mile Complex.... 31 F6
Korean Hot Stone BBQ.. 32 B1
Masala Hut................... 33 B5
Sungei Rd Laksa........... 34 D5
Tekka Centre................. 35 B5

🍸 DRINK
BluJaz Cafe 36 E7
Prince of Wales............. 37 C6
Thai Disco 38 F6

⭐ PLAY
Climb Asia 39 D3
DHL Balloon.................. 40 D8
Waterloo St Fortune
  Tellers........................ 41 C7

Please see over for map

tobacco) pipes mingles with the charcoal smoke along the dimly lit streets to give it a character all its own.

Towards the city centre, Bugis has been taken over by Singapore's largest street market, and is the place to go for cheap clothes, shoes and accessories.

👁 SEE

Little India is not renowned for the kind of attractions that fill brochures – the Colonial District has cornered the market on postcard sights – but it is a neighbourhood that warrants aimless wandering. Strolling through the narrow side streets with no fixed destination and watching life unfold is one of the great pleasures to be had here.

👁 KUAN IM THONG HOOD CHO TEMPLE
178 Waterloo St; 🕐 **6am-6.15pm;** Ⓜ **Bugis;** ♿
Dedicated to Kuan Yin, goddess of mercy, this is one of Singapore's busiest temples. Flower sellers, fortune tellers and incense-wielding devotees swarm around the entrance and rub the belly of the large bronze Buddha Maitreya nearby.

👁 SRI SRINIVASA PERUMAL TEMPLE
☎ **6298 5771; 397 Serangoon Rd;** 🕐 **6.30am-noon & 6-9pm;** Ⓜ **Farrer Park;** ♿
Dating from 1855, this is one of the city's most important temples.

If you're here in February for the Thaipusam Festival (p24), the procession of devotees, with spikes and skewers driven through their bodies, begins under the temple's *gopuram* (entrance tower).

👁 SRI VEERAMAKALIAMMAN TEMPLE
☎ **6293 4634; 141 Serangoon Rd;** 🕐 **8am-12.30pm & 4pm-8.30pm;** Ⓜ **Little India**
One of Little India's more colourful temples, this place is dedicated to the goddess Kali, bloodthirsty consort of Shiva, who is usually depicted wearing a necklace of skulls and disembowelling unfortunate humans.

GETTING THERE & AROUND
> **MRT** – The North East Line from Little India to Farrer Park gets you from one end of the area to the other.
> **Bus** – The 23, 64, 65, 66 and 147 run the length of Serangoon Rd. The 48 runs from Little India MRT on Bukit Timah Rd to the Arab Quarter (get off on Ophir Rd).

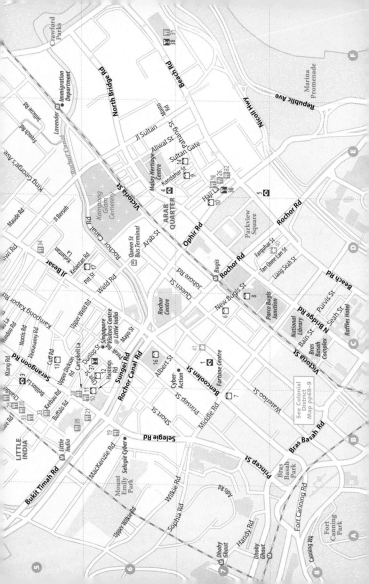

Visit Singapore's largest mosque, the grand Sultan Mosque

🕌 SULTAN MOSQUE

☎ 6293 4405; 3 Muscat St;
🕙 11am-4pm; Ⓜ Bugis

Singapore's largest mosque and the spiritual focal point for the neighbourhood since the days when it was the embarkation point for Mecca-bound pilgrims. The current magnificent, imposing building (designed, interestingly, by an Irishman) dates from 1928, but a mosque has stood there since 1825.

🛍 SHOP

Little India and the Arab Quarter are heaven for browsers and mall-haters – look, real shops, run by real shop owners, and barely a whiff of air-con or polished marble! Little India brims with gold shops, textiles, handicrafts, food, music and art. In the Arab Quarter, Arab St is well known for its textiles and carpets, pedestri-

BUSSORAH ST
A few years ago, it was decided that Bussorah St was the ideal location for an 'alternative lifestyle hub' (yes, almost nothing happens here by accident). While that vision was never quite realised, this tiled, tree-lined and pedestrianised strip is nevertheless one of the city's most appealing streets, filled with handicraft shops, a backpacker hostel and several cafés. Check out the eccentric **Grandfather's Collections** curio shop, the **Little Shophouse** next door, which specialises in the dying art of Peranakan beadwork, or the Javanese arts and crafts at **Melor's Curios**.

anised Bussorah St has become a mildly bohemian enclave of knick-knacks, galleries and spas, while the back street of Haji Lane houses some hip boutiques and secondhand shops. New Bugis St has been turned into a two-storey street market likely to swallow teenagers whole.

🛍 BUGIS ST MARKET
Street Market
Victoria St; 🕙 11am-10pm; Ⓜ **Bugis**
Once Singapore's most infamous sleaze pit, this is now its largest street market, filled with cheap clothes, shoes, accessories, manicurists, food stalls and, in a nod to its past, a sex shop. You'll even find (gasp) the occasional knock-off.

🛍 EDGE *Fashion*
☎ 6557 6557; 03, Parco Bugis Junction, **200 Victoria St;** 🕙 11am-9pm; Ⓜ **Bugis**
A thicket of local streetwear outlets wedged into a corner of Parco Bugis Junction, illustrating the revolving-door nature of Singapore fashion. Don't put off buying that T-shirt until tomorrow, because the shop may well have packed up and gone by the time you come back.

🛍 GOLDEN MILE COMPLEX
Food
5001 Beach Rd; 🕙 9am-9pm;
Ⓜ **Bugis, Lavender**
This is Thailand: the whole human circus wrapped up, packaged inside an unattractive shopping centre and transported to Singapore (minus the motorbikes running you down on the pavement). This is the

HAJI LANE
It's the kind of place you'd walk past without a second thought – a narrow, dingy lane with crumbling, graffiti-covered walls and no evident appeal. But Haji Lane is becoming a place of pilgrimage for Singapore's hipsters and fashionistas who insist on wearing originals from shops that don't use capital letters. Boutiques come and go rapidly, but try **dulcetfig** for retro dresses, **dion de cruz** and **Victoria JoMo** for street chic, **salad** for home accessories or the long-standing **House of Japan** for secondhand Japanese fashion.

LITTLE INDIA & THE ARAB QUARTER

place to come for Thai groceries, including all the essential roots, leaves and pastes you'll struggle to find anywhere else. Stay for lunch or dinner (see p93).

🏠 **INDIAN CANDYS** *Food*
01-16, Little India Arcade; 🕑 **9am-9pm;**
Ⓜ **Little India**

There are dozens of great Indian sweet shops in Little India, but we like this one because of the bad spelling and the grumpy old fellas behind the counter (though if you're pretty and female they may suddenly get a spring in their step).

Expect a riot of vibrant colours in Little India

🏠 INDIAN CLASSICAL MUSIC CENTRE *Music*
☎ 6291 0187; 26 Clive St; ⏱ 10am-8pm Mon-Sat, 10am-4pm Sun; Ⓜ Little India

A tiny shop filled with sitars, tabla and all manner of bells both wearable and shakeable. Buy CDs to play along to, or sign up for music lessons.

🏠 INDIAN HANDICRAFT CENTRE *Handicrafts, Furniture*
☎ 6392 0769; 2 Dalhousie Lane; ⏱ 9am-10pm; Ⓜ Little India

The best place to browse for all things homely and Indian, from cushions to statues to screens to furniture – this place has everything. A lot of larger items aren't on display, so if you're looking for something in particular, ask the friendly owner.

🏠 KHAN MOHAMED BHOY & SONS *Food*
☎ 6293 6191; 20 Cuff Rd; ⏱ 8am-8.30pm; Ⓜ Little India

You don't have to see this store to find it. Follow your nose to what may be the last traditional spice-grinding shop in Singapore. Plastic garbage bins full of dried bell chillies crowd the doorway, while inside you can take away big scoops of turmeric, cumin and fennel or order them freshly ground.

CURIOUCE?

For a peek at work being turned out by Singapore's young fashion designers, have a look inside the **Curiocity Gallery** (☎ 6334 6022; 38 Bencoolen St; ⏱ 10am-5pm; Ⓜ Bugis) run by the Nanyang Academy of Fine Arts. The industry is still young, but it's clear some promising talents are being unearthed in the new, creative Singapore.

🏠 MUSTAFA CENTRE *Department Store*
☎ 6295 5855; 145 Syed Alwi Rd; ⏱ 24hr; Ⓜ Farrer Park

A Singapore legend, as much cultural rite of passage as shopping experience, Mustafa's narrow aisles and tiny nooks have everything from electronics, clothing, toiletries, tacky clothes (lurid Bollywood shirts always make great presents), cheap DVDs, gold, moneychangers, a supermarket (it's *the* place to stock up on Indian spices and pickles) and sometimes half the population of Singapore.

🏠 SIM LIM SQ *IT, Mall*
☎ 6332 5839; 1 Rochor Canal Rd; ⏱ 11am-9pm; Ⓜ Bugis

A byword for all that is cut-price and geeky, Sim Lim is not for those uninitiated in the world of sim cards, RAM, motherboards and soundcards. If you know what you're doing, there are real bargains to be had, but the untutored are more likely to be taken for a ride. Hard bargaining is essential.

🏠 SUNGEI RD THIEVES MARKET *Street Market*

Sungei Rd, Weld Rd, Pasar Lane & Pitt St; ⏲ **10am-6pm;** Ⓜ **Little India, Bugis**

A true Singapore oddity, this collection of old geezers and dodgy characters splaying out random collections of used items on the pavement every day offers a peek into the underbelly of the city. Tennis shoes, mobile phones, watches, motorcycle helmets, old vinyl records, a builder's hard hat, a dinner jacket and a set of spanners were just a few of the items we saw on our last visit. Everyone expects the authorities to close it down any day, but somehow it continues to thrive.

🏠 TEKKA CENTRE *Textiles*

cnr Serangoon & Buffalo Rds; ⏲ **10am-9pm;** Ⓜ **Little India**

Once you've fought your way through the hawker centre and the rather lurid wet market (avoid it if you don't like severed sheep's heads), there's a whole floor of textile and sari shops on the first level – the cheapest place to pick up an Indian outfit. Prices are labelled, but bargaining is expected.

🍴 EAT

It hardly needs saying: the sheer wealth of superb Indian food here is overwhelming. Though still dominated by the cuisines of the south, a recent influx of North Indian professionals has seen a new wave of northern food hit the area. Down in the Arab Quarter, a renaissance in Middle Eastern eating is in full swing, while across Beach Rd, cheap Thai feasts await at the Golden Mile Complex.

🍴 AL-TAZZAG
Middle Eastern $

☎ **6295 5024; 24 Haji Lane;** ⏲ **11.30am-4am Mon-Sat, 4pm-4am Sun;** Ⓜ **Bugis;** ♿ 🧒 Ⓥ

Café Le Caire (p92) beats it for food, but Al-Tazzag wins the atmosphere competition. Set in the quiet back street of Haji Lane, this colourful café also spreads out along the five-foot ways, serving up meals, mint teas and *shisha* to Singapore's hipsters until the early hours. No alcohol – but boozy BluJaz Café (p94) is metres away.

🍴 ANANDA BHAVAN
Vegetarian $

☎ **6297 9522; Block 663, 01-10, Buffalo Rd;** ⏲ **7.30am-10pm;** Ⓜ **Little India;** ♿ Ⓥ 🧒

Little India specialises in unappealing fluoro-lit, plastic-table eateries that look more like burger joints; but swallow your aesthetic concerns and plunge into the wonderful North and South Indian veggie fare here – the set meals are truly enormous. There are other Little India outlets at Tekka Market, Selegie Rd and Syed Alwi Rd, opposite Mustafa Centre.

ANDHRA CURRY *Indian* $$

☎ 6296 3935; 41 Kerbau Rd;
🕐 11.30am-3.30pm & 6-10.30pm Mon-Fri, 11.30am-10.30pm Sat & Sun;
Ⓜ Little India; 👫 👶 Ⓥ

This no-frills, no-ceremony restaurant specialises in fiery recipes from the South Indian state of Andhra Pradesh. Attentive staff dish up Hyderabadi biryani (traditionally cooked in a dough-sealed pot), a very hot dry mutton curry

Visitors will find a stunning array of both fresh and cooked produce in Little India

CHANDER RD

Tucked behind its more illustrious Race Course Rd neighbour and almost completely undiscovered by visitors, Chander Rd is also a treasure chest of Indian food – often at much lower prices. Have a wander and see what takes your fancy, but **Ghandi** (☎ 6299 5343; 31 Chander Rd), **Masala Hut** (☎ 6341 5101; 21 Chander Rd) and **Chettinadu** (☎ 6291 7161; 41 Chander Rd) all do a good trade.

and large vegetarian thalis. Packed on Sundays.

🍴 ANJAPPAR *Indian* $$

☎ 6392 5545; www.anjappar.com.sg; 102 Syed Alwi Rd; 🕑 11.30am-11.30pm; Ⓜ Farrer Park; 🚻 🚹 Ⓥ

The two Little India outlets of this Chennai-based dynasty serve up outstanding Chettinaad cuisine, from the deep south of India. Our favourites are the mutton *uppu kari* and the chicken *nattu koli masala*, the latter guaranteed to have you gasping in blissful chilli heaven. The flagship branch is on Race Course Rd, but the service is better here.

🍴 BANANA LEAF APOLO *Indian* $$

☎ 6297 1595; 54-58 Race Course Rd; 🕑 10.30am-10.30pm; Ⓜ Little India; 🚹 Ⓥ

A popular stop on the tourist trail, but the uncompromisingly fiery food here has legions of fans both local and foreign, though the service can be poor. Offers wide range of Indian food, all served up on banana leaves, but most famous for its blistering fish-head curry, which will have you pouring with sweat and wondering why you ever thought such a dish would be disgusting.

🍴 CAFÉ LE CAIRE

Middle Eastern $

☎ 6292 0979; 29 Arab St; 🕑 11am-3am; Ⓜ Bugis; 🚻 🚹 Ⓥ

Blink and you'll miss it during the day, but at night this alcohol-free Egyptian café becomes a miniature scene, especially at weekends, colonising both sides of the street with tables and rugs, filled with lounging *shisha*-smokers and eager diners gorging on kebabs and superb dips. A must.

🍴 FRENCH STALL *French* $$

☎ 6299 3544; 544 Serangoon Rd; 🕑 noon-3pm & 6-10pm Tue-Sun; Ⓜ Farrer Park; 🚻 🚹

Set up by two–Michelin-star chef Xavier Le Henaff to debunk the notion that French food must be expensive, this unpretentious stall is a gem – great food, great desserts and great wine in a coffeeshop environment.

🍴 GAYATRI *Indian* $$

☎ 6291 1011; www.gayatrirestaurant .com; 122 Race Course Rd; 🕑 11.30am-10.30pm; Ⓜ Little India; 🚻 🚹 Ⓥ

Another popular restaurant specialising in fish-head curry and other South Indian specialities, but its relative lack of fame has ensured the service here is friendly and swift and far, far better than its Banana Leaf Apolo rival. Its fish-head curry is on par with the Banana Leaf and there are far fewer tourists.

GOLDEN MILE COMPLEX
Thai $$

5001 Beach Rd; 11am-10.30pm;
Bugis, Lavender
Singapore's Little Thailand. Forget all the fancy restaurants with their Buddha statues and cultural knick-knacks, if you want real Thai food, brave the stumbling drunken Isaan workers in this seedy old shopping centre for an evening of friendly service, cheap Singha and *sôm-tam* (papaya salad) like mother used to make. It's uniformly superb (the northeastern Thai food is best), but the Nong Khai Food & Beer Garden on the ground floor is particularly good. Complete the experience at Thai Disco 1 or 2 (see p94) afterwards.

KOREAN HOT STONE BBQ
Korean $$

6299 3866; 249 Beach Rd;
11.30pm-10.30pm; **Bugis;**
An alternative to the area's ubiquitous Middle Eastern fare, this is always packed with Singaporean

> **WATERLOO ST FORTUNE TELLERS**
> On the corner of Albert St and the Waterloo St pedestrian mall, not far from Bugis St Market, just up from the Kuan Im Thong Hood Cho Temple, you'll find a collection of Chinese fortune tellers waiting patiently at tables underneath umbrellas. Many speak no English, but some use translators and will happily forecast great riches for you for around $5 a pop. What, you mean you didn't know you had five children who are all destined to become rich?

diners at night, feasting on *kim chi* (pickled cabbage), hotpot and other Korean classics.

SUNGEI RD LAKSA *Laksa* $
01-100, Jin Shui Kopitiam, Jalan Besar;
9am-6pm; **Lavender**
Selected by the *Makansutra* street-food guru as Singapore's best laksa and who's to argue? Apparently this laksa master uses only charcoal to keep his precious gravy warm and, unlike other successful hawkers, refuses to open other branches. Get there around 11.30am or after 2pm to avoid the lunchtime rush.

TEKKA CENTRE
Hawker Centre $
cnr Serangoon & Buffalo Rds; 7am-11pm; **Little India;**
Queue up for biryani, *dosai* (South Indian savoury pancake), roti prata

and *teh tarik* (pulled tea), then wedge yourself into a table at this legendary hawker centre wrapped around the sloshed guts and hacked bones of the wet market.

▼ DRINK

▼ BLUJAZ CAFÉ *Pub*
☎ 6292 3800; 11 Bali Lane; ☼ noon-midnight Mon-Thu, noon-2am Fri, 4pm-2am Sat; Ⓜ Bugis; ♿
A beautiful old building, renovated as a bar and decorated in a decidedly eccentric bohemian style which, coupled with its location on the edge of the Arab Quarter and next to an artists' studio, makes it pretty much unique in Singapore. Live jazz downstairs on Monday, Friday and Saturday completes the mood.

▼ PRINCE OF WALES *Pub*
☎ 6299 0310; 101 Dunlop St; ☼ 9am-1am; Ⓜ Little India
Rough at the edges, knockabout Australian-style pub and beer garden, with scuffed wooden floors, Gippsland Pale on tap, acoustic strummers and live bands, and appropriately laconic blokes behind the bar. A slightly surreal enclave of non-Indians amid the Sunday evening Little India melee.

▼ THAI DISCO *Nightclub*
☎ 6295 1611; 02-85, Golden Mile Complex, 5001 Beach Rd; ☼ 8pm-3am

Mon-Fri, 8pm-4am Sat, 6pm-3am Sun; Ⓜ Lavender
Thoroughly raucous, slightly seedy and heartily drunken – it's a Thai disco! The house band, featuring scantily dressed female singers and heavily hair-gelled male heart-throbs, play danceable rock classics at high volume, while admirers buy garlands to place around their necks. You're likely to be the only tourist in here, but no-one seems to care.

★ PLAY

★ CLIMB ASIA
☎ 6292 7701; www.climb-asia.com; 60 Tessensohn Rd; admission before/after 5pm $6/8, membership $40; ☼ 5-11pm Mon, 10am-11pm Tue-Fri, 10am-9pm Sat & Sun
Highly professional climb centre with a challenging series of indoor walls, a realistic outdoor wall and a boulder cave. Good spot to get the lowdown on climbing spots around the region.

★ DHL BALLOON
☎ 6338 6877; Tan Quee Lan St; adult/child $23/13; ☼ 11am-9.30pm; Ⓜ Bugis
Though it threatens to be overshadowed by the Singapore Flyer (p73), the views from this tethered helium balloon, which rises an unsettling 150m into the air, give you a more close-up view of the city. It's particularly dramatic after dark.

Selena Tan
Performer, Dim Sum Dollies

Best place in Singapore to catch theatre outside the mainstream? The Arts House (Map pp68–9) or the Drama Centre Black Box (Map pp68–9). Theatreworks (Map pp68–9) also has a space down on Mohamed Sultan Rd and the Substation (Map pp68–9) is trying to rejuvenate itself. **Most underrated theatre company?** Cake. They create all their own work and they're very 'out there'. Instead of working to scripts they have a broad idea, then bring actors together and workshop productions. **Favourite theatre to perform in?** Esplanade (p67). **Best after-show late-night bar?** Harry's at the Esplanade. **Best tip for theatre-lovers coming to Singapore?** Because there's nothing regular and theatre is very sporadic, people should check Sistic (www.sistic.com.sg) – all tickets for productions are channelled through them, even the fringe performances.

>SENTOSA

Sentosa has come a long way in a short time. It's not so long since Singapore's self-styled pleasure isle was a national joke, its attractions either ageing and fading, or depressing and deserted flops, lampooned by locals, tourists and guidebooks as feeble and kitsch.

Elements of its tasteless past are still evident, but under the inspired leadership of a now-departed American executive, Sentosa has been reborn. Top-notch hotels, two world-class golf courses, new or upgraded attractions, excellent restaurants, trendy beach bars, dance parties, hordes of young Singaporeans on the beaches, an exclusive residential marina development and, not least, a vast casino resort and Universal Studios theme park due to open in 2010.

The sights don't come cheap, but lying on the beach or taking a hike or a bike ride along one of the island's nature trails costs nothing more than the entrance fee.

Sentosa is in, and suddenly it's no longer so embarrassing to announce you had fun there, though there's a distinct feeling the development is going too far and the intended beachy vibe is being submerged.

SENTOSA

◉ SEE
Cineblast 1 B2
Dolphin Lagoon.................2 C3
Fort Siloso 3 A1
Images of Singapore 4 B2
Sentosa 4D Magix ....(see 1)
Songs of the Sea...........5 B2
The Flying Trapeze 6 A2
Underwater World 7 A2

🍴 EAT
Coastes 8 B2
Il Lido................................9 D4
Samundar.........................10 C3
Suburbia...........................11 C3
The Cliff............................12 C3

🍸 DRINK
Café del Mar 13 B2

Cool Deck.........................14 A2
KM8 ....15 D4

⭐ PLAY
Sentosa Golf Club..........16 D4
Sentosa Luge..................17 B2
Sentosa Skyride 18 B2

See Southwest
Singapore
Map pp130–1

Pulau
Keppel

Keppel Harbour Terminal

Keppel Harbour

Cable Car
Towers

Cable Car

World
Trade
Centre

Monorail

Harbourfront

Vivocity

Ferry
Terminal

Gateway Ave

Brani Terminal Road P

Brani Terminal Ave

Causeway
Bridge

Visitor
Arrival
Centre

Pulau Brani

St 6

St 8

6–15

10–15

Selat
Sengkir

Buran
Darat

Serapong Hill Rd

Mt Serapong

Serapong
Golf Course

Tanjong
Golf Course

Allanbrooke Rd

Bukit Manis Rd

Tanjong Beach

Palawan Beach

Artillery Ave

Jetty Rd

Sky Tower
Merlion

Car Rd

Nature Trail

Cable Car Rd

Mt Emblah
(62m)

Siloso Rd

Siloso
Beach

Strait of
Singapore

N

0   400 m
0   0.2 miles

GETTING THERE & AROUND

Aside from getting a cab straight across – the fastest option – there are several dedicated methods of crossing the harbour. Once on the island, a series of colour-coded bus services and a beach tram – routes for which are laid out on the free visitors map – shuttle people around the island.

> **Cable Car** (regular car adult/child $11.90/6.50, glass-bottom car $18/11; 8.30am to 9pm) Board at World Trade Centre or Mount Faber.
> **Sentosa Bus** (tickets $3; 7am to midnight Sunday to Thursday, 7am to 12.30am Friday and Saturday) Runs between HarbourFront bus interchange and the Beach Station. Buy tickets at HarbourFront.
> **Sentosa Express** (tickets $3; 7am to midnight) Board at Vivocity Shopping Centre.
> **SIA Hop-On** (www.singaporeair.com/hop-on; adult/child $12/6, SIA passengers $3; 9am to 7.30pm) Stops at major shopping malls and hotels in the city.

◉ SEE

There are enough sights and activities on Sentosa to keep you occupied for a couple of days, though most people who aren't staying in the island's hotels cram whatever they can into a single day. All the attractions are operated under the Sentosa management umbrella and information on any of them can be obtained from the island hotline (☎ 1800 736 8672) or website (www.sentosa.com.sg).

◉ CINEBLAST

adult/child $16/9.50; 🕙 **10am-9pm;** ♿
Simulation ride that straps you into a chair and tricks your mind into thinking it's being flung through canyons, propelled down rapids, shot up high mountains and other nausea-inducing experiences.

◉ FORT SILOSO

adult/child $8/5; 🕙 **10am-6pm;** ♿
Preserved British coastal fort that proved famously useless when the Japanese stormed Singapore from the north in WWII. Documentaries, artefacts, animatronics and recreated historical scenes will absorb history buffs, while their kids tug them towards the exits.

◉ IMAGES OF SINGAPORE

adult/child $10/7; 🕙 **9am-7pm;** ♿
Thoroughly reworked interactive panorama of the island's history, going back to the 14th century and featuring recreations and the ubiquitous life-size models Singapore's attractions love so dearly. Despite some inevitable political spin and tacky merchandising, it's enjoyable.

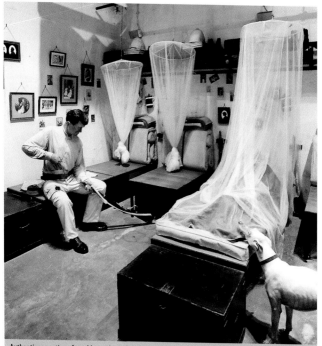

Authentic recreation of an old army barracks at Fort Siloso

SENTOSA 4D MAGIX
adult/child $16/9.50; **10am-9pm;**
Now a global theme park standard; somehow its movies in which things fly past your nose and spray water in your face never lose their appeal. Good fun.

SONGS OF THE SEA
adult & child $6; **7.40pm & 8.40pm;**
Extravagant light and sound show set around a replica Malay fisherman's village. The location and the visual effects are stunning but the Lloyd Webber–esque theatricality veers towards the cheesy.

📷 UNDERWATER WORLD & DOLPHIN LAGOON

adult/child $19.90/12.70;
⏱ **9am-9pm;** ♿

Ageing slightly, and set to be completely eclipsed by the world's largest oceanarium under construction at the island's new casino resort, kids will nonetheless get a kick out of the giant spider crabs, sting rays and impossibly lovable manatee. Tickets include entry to the Dolphin Lagoon show further along the coast.

🍴 EAT

When it came to food, Sentosa used to be a saturated fat-laden hell of junk-food outlets and stalls selling bad, overpriced versions of Singapore hawker staples. How things change. There is now good food pretty much everywhere and among the medals Sentosa pins on its chest are a couple of the city's best restaurants.

🍴 COASTES *European* $$

☎ **6274 9668; Siloso Beach;** ⏱ **10am-10pm Mon-Thu, 11am-1am Fri, 11am-1am Sat, 9am-10pm Sun;** ♿ 🚼

Best of the Sentosa beach eateries, serving up excellent pizzas, pasta and curries to a relaxed crowd. Grab a rustic table under the pergola, or look louche on the sun loungers. It's not exclusively for the hip, tanned and beautiful, as the thumping music suggests.

🍴 IL LIDO *Italian* $$$

☎ **6866 1977; www.il-lido.com; Sentosa Golf Club, Bukit Manis Rd;** ⏱ **11.30am-2.30pm, 6.30pm-11pm;** ♿ 🆅

Thoroughly outstanding Italian restaurant, with mouthwatering views across the Strait of Singapore, Il Lido screams out for a special occasion and the best outfit in the wardrobe. Offers modern, classic and vegetarian menus, plus one of the best wine lists in the city. Oh, and there's a yacht for private-dining occasions, a snip at $3000 for dinner.

🍴 SAMUNDAR *Indian* $$

☎ **6276 8891; www.samundar.com.sg; 85 Palawan Beach Walk;** ⏱ **10.30am-10pm Mon-Thu, 10.30am-11pm Fri-Sun;** ♿ 🚼 🆅

Avoid the air-con inside and grab an outdoor table, a few beers and order up big from the tandoor menu at this beachside beauty. The North Indian bias suggests it's aimed squarely at the legions of Indian tourists on Sentosa. Features an extensive vegetarian menu.

🍴 SUBURBIA *Wine Bar* $$

☎ **6376 5938; www.suburbia.com.sg;** ⏱ **3-10pm Mon-Thu, 3-10.30pm Fri & Sat;** ♿

STAYING ON SENTOSA

Bali it ain't, but waking up on Sentosa can still put you in the holiday mood. Top of the pile are **The Sentosa** (☎ 6275 0331; www.thesentosa.com), with fabulous rooms and junior suites, and the **Amara Sanctuary** (☎ 6825 3888; www.amarasanctuary.com), whose private villas come with private plunge pools and outdoor baths. One rung down are the **Treasure Resort** (☎ 6271 2002; www.treasure-resort.com), housed in a restored 1940s building, and the **Rasa Sentosa** (☎ 6235 1665; www.shangri-la.com), a beachfront family resort that looks like a banana-shaped cruise ship. At the budget end are the chalets of the **Costa Sands Resort** (☎ 6275 1034; www.costasands.com.sg). As for the **Siloso Beach Resort**, we say don't bother – the rooms we saw smelled strongly of mildew, which may have something to do with them laying carpet in the open air.

This is a cool, modern wine bar and restaurant in a lush garden setting. Sure, it doesn't have the sea views of other Sentosa competitors, and the building looks a bit like a university science block, but at night it's a perfect spot to sit outside and down a bottle or two.

🍴 THE CLIFF Seafood $$$

☎ 6275 0331; www.thesentosa.com; 2 Bukit Manis Rd; ⏱ 6.30-11pm (last orders 9.30pm); ♿

With its stunning views, a breezy clifftop outdoor setting and a superb seafood selection, this restaurant rivals Il Lido for romance. Make the experience even better by choosing to retire to one of the hotel's junior suites after dinner. With all those oysters around, you might need it. Definitely one of Singapore's best spots to eat.

🍸 DRINK

Sentosa has made a conscious effort to generate a cool edge to its image to attract the city's affluent, fashionable youth. Beach raves have been a wild success, though there has been talk of stopping them, and the beachfront Balearic-style clubs attract legions of the tanned.

🍸 CAFÉ DEL MAR

Bar, Nightclub

☎ 6235 1296; www.cafedelmar .com.sg; 40 Siloso Beach Walk; ⏱ 11am-1am Mon-Thu, 11am-4am Fri, 10am-4am Sat, 10am-1am Sun; ♿

Café del Mar evidently objects to the idea of a quiet day at the beach, but at night after the deafened day-trippers in the vicinity have crept home this Ibiza-inspired bar comes into its own.

NEIGHBOURHOODS

SENTOSA

Day beds and pastel pouffes on the sand, a poolside bar, Saturday bikini foam parties, DJs...you get the picture.

COOL DECK *Bar*
☎ 6279 3273; Siloso Beach; ⏰ 11am-9pm Mon-Fri, 11am-11pm Sat & Sun

The solution for anyone who wants a sea-front drink but doesn't feel like a lychee martini on a sun lounger in the company of 'DJ Deckster feat. Bassdamania' at KM8 further down the beach. The perfect spot for a beer and a moan about today's youth.

You can expect plenty of sun, sea, booze and bikinis at Café del Mar (p101)

⏻ KM8 *Bar, Nightclub*
☎ 6274 2288; www.km8.com.sg; 120 Tanjong Beach Walk; ☽ noon-10pm Mon, 11am-10pm Tue-Thu, 11am-1am Fri-Sun; ♿

With horns locked with Café del Mar in the Ibiza-lookalike contest, KM8 just about holds its own, despite being hampered by a less convenient location and earlier closing times. On the plus side, it's more laid-back, less crowded and the DJs are less intrusive in the daytime.

⭐ PLAY

✪ SENTOSA GOLF CLUB
☎ 6275 0090; www.sentosagolf .com; Bukit Manis Rd; Tanjong course weekday/weekend $280/400, Serapong course $310/450; ☽ tee-off sessions 7.35-9.20am & 12.45-2.25pm

Boasting two lush, immaculate championship-level courses, Sentosa has successfully pitched (pardon the pun) itself as one of the island's most prestigious clubs. Book well in advance.

✪ SENTOSA LUGE & SKYRIDE
ride or chairlift $9, four rides or chairlifts $26; ☽ 10am-9.30pm

Imported from New Zealand, so you know it must involve reckless endangerment, the luge is 60 seconds of racing through hairpin bends and bone-shaking straights carved through the forest. The chairlift back up offers views so good you don't need to pay for a visit up the Sky Tower nearby.

✪ THE FLYING TRAPEZE
Trapeze School; per swing $10, three swings $20; ☽ 4-6pm Tue-Fri, 4-7pm Sat & Sun

Do kids still dream of running away to the circus? Perhaps the lure of mounting the trapeze still runs deep – deeper hopefully than the desire to wear a lycra bodysuit.

>EASTERN SINGAPORE

Because of its lack of obvious tourist attractions, the eastern side of Singapore rarely sees foreign visitors, despite boasting some of its oldest neighbourhoods and a strong claim as the city's culinary capital.

The twin historical districts of Geylang and Katong, both traditionally Malay quarters, have very different characteristics. Geylang is the notorious centre of Singapore's red-light trade, only coming alive late in the evening, when its even-numbered *lorong* (side streets) teem with mostly Chinese men and prostitutes, and its back alleys host illegal gambling tables. Despite this, many locals say Geylang has the best local food.

Further east, Katong was also a centre of the Peranakan community, whose ornate shophouses line the area around Joo Chiat Rd, another excellent hunting ground for food, though signs of gentrification are creeping in.

Lining the shore is the large East Coast Park, an urban seaside oasis.

EASTERN SINGAPORE

SEE

CHANGI MEMORIAL & CHAPEL

☎ 6214 2451; www.changimuseum.com; 1000 Upper Changi Rd North; admission free; ⏱ 9.30am-5pm; Ⓜ Tanah Merah, then bus 2

The destruction of the original site to make way for prison expansion was an affront to many POWs who suffered terribly at the hands of the Japanese, but give some credit to the authorities for moving the memorial elsewhere. The photographs, letters and drawings graphically illustrate the horror of WWII and the chapel itself is a moving recreation of the kind built by the prisoners from the period.

KATONG ANTIQUES HOUSE

☎ 6345 8544; 208 East Coast Rd; ⏱ 11am-6.30pm (call for appointment); 🚌 10, 14

A rare opportunity to see a preserved Peranakan house, filled with original, or carefully restored antiques, from jewellery to furniture and, of course, beadwork. The owner is a true enthusiast.

EAT

Welcome to the heartland of Singapore cuisine. The dazzling development that has swamped much of Singapore has bypassed most of Geylang and Katong, where rough and ready hawker centres and coffeeshops dominate. East Coast Park is less intimidating, with its popular outdoor sea-front 'food village' and famous seafood centre.

328 KATONG LAKSA

Hawker Stall $

☎ 9732 8163; 216 East Coast Rd; ⏱ 8.30am-9pm; Ⓜ Eunos, then walk; 🚌 10, 12, 14, 32; ♿

One day maybe someone will unearth an ancient scroll describing the original Katong laksa, and the unending dispute between the neighbouring stalls here over who was first will finally end. Until then, you won't go wrong with the rich and creamy offering here. Was it first? Do we care? The expanding size and opening of new branches would suggest it's the most popular, or at least the most business-savvy.

A STROLL ALONG THE BEACH

If Beach Rd sounds like a strange name for a road several hundred metres from the sea, it really isn't. Not so long ago, every inch of land beyond it didn't exist. In fact, the country used to be a staggering 135 sq km smaller – and there are plans for another 100 sq km of expansion in the future via further land reclamation.

🍴 AWFULLY CHOCOLATE *Café* $

☎ 6345 2190; 01-26, Katong Mall; 112 East Coast Rd; 🕙 10.30am-9pm; 🚍 10, 14

This is a dangerous establishment. It only offers three cakes (chocolate, banana chocolate and rum cherry chocolate) and one ice cream, but they are all of the variety that produce decidedly sexual exclamations from females who eat them.

🍴 CHILLI PADI *Peranakan* $$

☎ 6275 1002; 11 Joo Chiat Pl; 🕙 11.30am-2.30pm, 5.30-10.30pm; Ⓜ Eunos, then walk; ♿

Homestyle Nonya cooking, set in a row of picturesque shophouses in the heart of Peranakan country. Dig into some fiery, sour *asam* (tamarind) fish head, the range of classic chicken dishes, or the *sambal* (spicy shrimp paste) seafood. Its success has spawned other branches and a range of home-cook pastes.

🍴 EAST COAST LAGOON FOOD VILLAGE *Hawker Centre* $

East Coast Park Service Rd; 🕙 10.30am-11pm; Ⓜ Bedok, then taxi, 🚍 401 from Bedok MRT (weekends only); ♿

Certainly there can be few hawker centres with a better location. Tramp barefoot off the beach, order up some *satay* (meat skewers cooked over a flame), seafood, or the uniquely Singaporean *satay bee hoon* (rice vermicelli) from Meng Kee at stall 17 (get there

GETTING THERE & AROUND

> **MRT** – The East–West Line runs along the fringe of East Coast.
> **Bus** – 2, 13, 21 and 26 run along Sims Ave through Geylang. 10 and 14 run along East Coast Rd and Upper East Coast Rd, while 15, 31 and 76 service Marine Parade Rd.

before 6pm, or you'll end up in a long queue).

🍴 ENG SENG COFFEESHOP *Hawker Centre* $

247/249 Joo Chiat Pl; 🕙 5pm-9pm; Ⓜ Eunos, then bus 155; ♿

Known all over the island for its black-pepper crab (though – surprise, surprise – many dispute its pre-eminence) the queues start even before 5pm. Evidently people duck out of work early to eat here. The crab is worth a wait, but if you're hungry and impatient the BBQ seafood stall also has several loyal fans.

🍴 GUAN HOE SOON *Peranakan* $$

☎ 6344 2761; 214 Joo Chiat Rd; 🕙 11am-2.30pm & 6-9.30pm Wed-Mon; Ⓜ Eunos, then bus 155; ♿

Claims to be the oldest Peranakan restaurant in Singapore and makes the most of its status as Lee Kuan Yew's favourite, but in a city rich

NEIGHBOURHOODS

EASTERN SINGAPORE

FOOD WARS

In a country as opinionated about food as Singapore, it's not surprising that regular wars break out between hawkers claiming to be the best, the original, the most famous, the only...some disputes have even ended in legal action. The most renowned was over Katong Laksa – dubbed by the media as the unresolved 'laksa wars', after which 328 Katong Laksa, Original Katong Laksa (also known as Marine Parade Laksa) and the somewhat adamantly named Janggut The Original Katong Laksa Since 1950 were all still standing.

in food mythology and boastful claims, this kind of information cuts little ice. It's the food that does the talking – and the food here shouts pretty loud. Try the *sotong sambal* (squid in *sambal*) or, our favourite Peranakan dish, *ayam buah keluak* (chicken cooked with black nut).

🍴 JOO CHIAT PLACE FRIED KWAY TEOW *Chinese* $

1 Joo Chiat Pl; 🕒 9.30am-10.30pm; Ⓜ Eunos, then bus 155; ♿ ⛲
Home of renowned fried *kway teow* (flat rice noodles), the recipe for which dates back to the pre-WWII era. The sibling owners have undergone a few location shifts, but this seems to be a permanent home. Closed on alternate Tuesdays.

🍴 JUST GREENS VEGETARIAN *Vegetarian* $

☎ 6345 0069; 49/51 Joo Chiat Pl; 🕒 8am-10pm; Ⓜ Eunos, then taxi or walk; ♿ Ⓥ
You know the vegetarian food must be good when you're lined up alongside Buddhist monks (queuing for food is a good sign). Pick from the menu in the dining room, or choose from the selections at the door and take them inside.

🍴 MANGO TREE *Indian* $$

☎ 6442 8655; 1000 East Coast Parkway; 🕒 noon-2.30pm & 6.30-10.30pm; Ⓜ Eunos, then taxi, 🚌 401 from Bedok MRT (weekends only)
Tiny, elegant, cosy beachfront restaurant specialising in food from Kerala and Goa. The best spot is outside on the small deck, where you can catch the breeze, though the atmosphere is mildly spoiled by the bars sandwiching it either side.

🍴 NO SIGNBOARD SEAFOOD *Seafood* $$

☎ 6842 3415; 414 Geylang Rd; 🕒 noon-2am; Ⓜ Aljunied; ♿ ⛲
Legends of hawkers-turned-millionaires abound in Singapore, and few are more irresistible than this (see boxed text, p110). The fame of the white-pepper crab here has helped spawn five branches around the city, but this is the original restaurant – and it

¶¶ KF Seetoh
Hawker food guru, publisher of Makansutra *food guide*

Four must-try Singapore dishes and where to have them? Chicken rice from Tian Tian at Maxwell Rd Hawker Centre (p59), laksa from Sungei Rd Laksa (p93) at Jin Shui Kopitiam, fish-head curry at Banana Leaf Apolo (p92) and *char kway teow* (flat rice noodles, clams and eggs fried in chilli and black-bean sauce) from Outram Park Fried Kway Teow at Hong Lim Complex (p58). **Best place to take a date for dinner?** For romantic atmosphere, Il Lido (p100) on Sentosa for top end, Gluttons Bay at the Esplanade (p67) for midrange or East Coast Lagoon Food Village (p107) for budget. **Best places for a seafood feast?** Sin Huat Seafood Restaurant (p110) on Geylang Lorong 35 – have the crab *bee hoon*, *gong gong* and 'MRT' prawns, Long Beach Seafood Map p105; ☎ 6445 8833; www.longbeachseafood.com.sg; 1018 East Coast Parkway; ⏱ 11am-3pm, 5pm-12.30am) at East Coast for black-pepper crab or Matter Rd Seafood at Old Airport Rd Food Centre (p110) for white-pepper crab or chilli crab.

stays open later than the other branches, which are at East Coast Seafood Centre, Katong, Vivocity and the Esplanade.

🍴 OLD AIRPORT RD FOOD CENTRE *Hawker Centre* $

Block 51, Old Airport Rd; 🕑 **10am-late;** Ⓜ **Aljunied, then taxi;** ♿ 🚼 Ⓥ
One of the great things about eating in Singapore is that the most unappealing-looking places often house the most revered hawkers. This hidden nook boasts Matter Rd Seafood (sign is misspelled, but famous for white-pepper crab), Toa Payoh Rojak and the much-beloved fried Hokkien prawn noodle.

🍴 SIN HUAT SEAFOOD RESTAURANT *Seafood* $$$

☎ **6744 9755; Lorong 35, Geylang Rd;** 🕑 **11am-late;** Ⓜ **Aljunied, then walk;** ♿
Perhaps the most famous seafood joint in Singapore – and certainly the priciest hawker food. Chef Danny Lim is renowned internationally for his crab *bee hoon* (rice noodles), yet Sin Huat is determinedly grungy and its fame seems to have inspired some desultory, if not rude, service. They know people will keep flocking in, so they're not too bothered. If you want to eat sooner rather than later, try something else, such as the *gong gong* (whelks) or so-called 'MRT' prawns.

COOKING UP A STORM

If you learn how to cook Singapore-style, you won't need to come back! Classes run from two to four hours; some are hands-on, some are instruction only. Call for bookings and schedules.

> **at-sunrice GlobalChef Academy** (Map pp68–9; ☎ 6336 3307; www.at-sunrice.com; Fort Canning Centre, Fort Canning Park; classes $35-135; Ⓜ Dhoby Ghaut) Half-day classes with a spicy hands-on emphasis.

> **Cookery Magic** (Map p105; ☎ 6348 9667; www.cookerymagic.com; Haig Rd, Katong; classes $50-75; Ⓜ Paya Lebar) Ruqxana's classes for beginners in her own home, on an ecofarm or in a kampong (village) house on Pulau Ubin.

> **Coriander Leaf** (Map pp68–9; ☎ 6732 3354; www.corianderleaf.com; 02-03, 3A Merchant Court, River Valley Rd; classes from $110; Ⓜ Clarke Quay) Pan-Asian and Euro delights for small groups. See also p74.

> **Raffles Culinary Academy** (Map pp68–9; ☎ 6412 1256; www.raffleshotel.com; 02-17, Raffles Hotel, 1 Beach Rd; classes $65-130; Ⓜ City Hall) Chinese, Indian and Thai cuisine lessons straight from Raffles' kitchens.

> **Shermay's Cooking School** (Map pp118–19; ☎ 6479 8442; www.shermay.com; Block 43, 03-64, Jl Merah Saga, Chip Bee Gardens, Holland Village; classes $69-139; 🚌 7, 61, 77) Singaporean, Peranakan and chocolate are Shermay's faves!

THE LEGEND OF NO SIGNBOARD

The irony of having a 30-ft neon sign emblazoned with crustaceans will probably not escape diners at No Signboard Seafood – if they're not too busy gorging on its famous white-pepper crab. Evidently this hugely successful chain started as a nameless stall under Madam Ong Kim Hoi at the Mattar Rd Hawker Centre. When city officials wanted her to register her business under a title, she couldn't think of what to call it. The story goes that the now-famous name was suggested to the stumped Madam Ong by a well-known actor, who was a loyal customer.

VANSH Indian $$

☎ 6345 4466; 2 Stadium Walk; ⏰ noon-2.30pm, 6-11pm; Ⓜ Kallang, then taxi; Ⓖ Ⓥ

An unusual Indian restaurant, in that it's ditched the usual Indian décor in favour of an eye-catching modern design with recessed, cushion-laden seating, Vansh's take on the cuisine is equally impressive. The tandoor offerings are superb – or go on Sundays for all-you-can-eat kebabs and beer.

YONG HE EATING HOUSE
Hawker Centre $

☎ 6745 5682; Lorong 27 Geylang Rd; ⏰ 24hr; Ⓜ Aljunied, then walk; Ⓥ

Despite the fear of being spotted in Geylang at night, people flock to this all-night joint for its famous hot soya-bean milk, sweet bean-curd desserts and pork floss, though it's a bit too close to the sleaze for some.

DRINK

BARK CAFÉ *Cafe, Bar*

☎ 6545 4118; 1000 Upper Changi Rd North; ⏰ noon-12.30am Mon-Thu, till 1.30am Fri-Sun; Ⓜ Tanah Merah, then bus 2; Ⓖ

A relaxed, easygoing café right next door to the Changi Chapel, the Bark stays fairly low-key even on weekend nights, with a friendly crowd of mainly local residents enjoying the outdoor breeze, pool table, ample beers and excellent local (and international) food. The 'red plum soda' is evidently of some repute.

BERNIE'S BFD *Pub*

☎ 6244 4434; 1000 East Coast Parkway; ⏰ 4pm-2am Mon-Thu, 4pm-3am Fri, noon-3am Sat, noon-2am Sun; Ⓜ Eunos, then taxi, 🚌 401 from Bedok MRT (weekends only); Ⓖ

Saloon bar popular with expats, taking full advantage of the sea breezes and its seaside location, but retaining the dimly lit, dark-wood interior serious boozers require. There's live music most nights.

BLOOIE'S ROADHOUSE *Pub*

☎ 6442 0030; 49 Jl Tua Kong; ⏰ 11.30am-midnight Sun-Thu, 11.30am-1am Fri & Sat; 🚌 14; Ⓖ

Though hidden up a suburban side street in the heart of the affluent Siglap district, this jovial, rough-hewn bar feels like it should be facing a beach (or, apparently, a North American highway), with a rustic outdoor area, live music, hearty pub food and a boozy crowd.

☐ CHARLIE'S CORNER *Pub*

☎ 6542 0867; 01-08, Changi Village Hawker Centre, 2 Changi Village Rd; ⏲ 11am-2.30pm, 6-11pm Mon-Sat; Ⓜ Tanah Merah, then bus 2; ♿

Absorbing the languid Changi Village vibe, Charlie's has been around forever, dishing up Western food to the residents in this hidden corner of the island. The food isn't fantastic, but the huge range of beers can detain you for hours. Pop in after a visit to Pulau Ubin (see boxed text, p114).

☆ PLAY

☆ GALLOP STABLE *Horse Riding*

☎ 6583 9665; 61 Pasir Ris Green; rides $10-60; ⏲ 8-11am, 2-7pm Tue-Sun; Ⓜ Pasir Ris; ♿

One for the kids – stables and a paddock surrounded by trees in Pasir Ris Park. Where the nippers can take an 800m ride led by a trainer or, if they know how to ride, take a canter themselves for $40 to $60. Parents can watch proudly from the café, or take

part themselves. There are facilities for disabled riders, but call ahead.

☆ PASIR RIS PARK *Park*

Pasir Ris Dr 3; ⏲ 24hr; Ⓜ Pasir Ris

Heartlands Singapore is not all housing estates and hawker centres. You'll see few tourists in this superb seafront park, complete with a maze park, playgrounds, fishing pond, bike, rollerblade and kayak rental, horse riding (see left) and a pristine 5-hectare mangrove reserve ringed with boardwalks and bird-watcher's aerie. Of course, there are also eating options. Combine with Wild

RIDING THE COAST ROAD

One of the most pleasurable ways to pass a weekday afternoon (don't do this at weekends) is to cycle the length of East Coast Park. Pick up a bike at the **Marine Cove** rental station, go west past the surprisingly thick woods to the beginning of the path, then do a U-turn and head for Changi. The cycle path winds through gardens, nature reserves, restaurant strips, the **Ski 360°** lagoon, the **East Coast Lagoon Food Village**, **Bedok jetty** (check the little fisherman's camp next to it), past the **PA Sea Sports Centre**, then over a canal and past a quiet beach, where you can sit and watch the jets roaring right overhead as they come in to land at Changi Airport.

Fancy sliding down a three-storey-high half-pipe at the Wild Wild Wet theme park?

Wild Wet (right) for a family day out with a difference.

⭐ SKI 360° *Cable Ski*
☎ 6442 7318; www.ski360degree
.com; 1206A East Coast Parkway; per hr weekdays/weekends $32/42; ⏲ 10am-10pm Mon-Fri, 9am-midnight Sat & Sun; Ⓜ Bedok, then bus 401 (weekends only), 🚌 196, 197

What better way to cool off than to strap on some water skis, a kneeboard or a wakeboard and get dragged around a lagoon on the end of a cable? OK, you could just go swimming, but where's the fun in that? Best visited on weekday mornings, when there's usually hardly anyone there – unless a school party happens to drop by. The pose quotient goes through the roof at weekends.

⭐ WILD WILD WET *Theme Park*
☎ 6581 9135; www.wildwildwet.com; adult/child $12.90/8.80; ⏲ 1-7pm Mon & Wed-Fri, 10am-8pm Sat, Sun & school holidays; Ⓜ Pasir Ris

Part of the mushrooming Downtown East leisure complex, this water park doesn't boast the spectacular slides of its international rivals, but it's still lots of fun. Highlight is the unnerving Slide-Up, which involves pairs of people being folded into a rubber dinghy and pushed into a three-storey-high half-pipe. Weekdays are best, unless it's a school holiday. At weekends you can combine Wild Wild Wet with a visit to the **Escape Theme Park** (☎ 6581 9112; www.escapethemepark.com; adult/child $16.50/8.30), though the ageing rides will not impress kids accustomed to a diet of Disneyland and similar extravaganzas.

NEIGHBOURHOODS

EASTERN SINGAPORE

WORTH THE TRIP

Pulau Ubin (Map p115) is the Singapore that development left behind – a languid, ramshackle island of few people and fewer cars, small villages, forests, fish farms, quiet country lanes, old quarries and plantations.

More akin to rural Malaysia than Singapore (if you have a mobile phone, you'll even get a message welcoming you to Malaysia), locals pour over here at weekends, filling the belching old bumboats that chug across the channel ($2 each way, leaves when full; operates 6am-8pm) from Changi Point Ferry Terminal to the island jetty, to ride bikes along the narrow lanes and dirt tracks, dodging scurrying monitors, wild boar and sunbathing snakes.

Weekdays is the best time, when you'll have the island virtually to yourself. Docking at the jetty, where men fish from rocks and skeletal pilings jut from the water, is like entering another country. If you've come by cab from downtown Singapore, it's quite a jolt – the pace suddenly shifts into first gear, or even neutral.

Turn right at the end of the jetty to a small **information kiosk**, detailing Ubin's fauna and offering nuggets of history. Left from the jetty is the tiny village, where you can hire a mountain bike for between $4 and $10 per day (give them a thorough test – many lack adequate brakes and functional gears).

West of the village you'll pass the Pekan Quarry, fenced off to deter explorers. Keep heading west and you'll cross a bridge over a tidal inlet and hit Ubin Quarry on the right and the **Kampong Ubin Resort** (☎ 6388 8388; chalets from $180), which has remodelled itself as an adventure destination and spa. There's a decent seafood restaurant for lunch, though food is cheaper in the village.

An almost hidden track to the right of the resort leads to a gap in the fence, where you can clamber through and sit by the quarry edge.

Further on, the road forks. Right leads to the northern shore. Left leads to the strange **German Girl Shrine**, housed in a yellow hut under a tree to the left, where some Chinese devotees come to pray to the spirit of a young German who died there during WWII.

North and east of the main village you'll pass **prawn farms** and old plantations. In the north is **Noordin Beach**, where you can camp for free (though it's none too appealing). At the extreme east is **Tanjong Chek Jawa**, a pristine mangrove threaded with boardwalks.

Back in the village, reward yourself with a seafood feast and beers at **Season Live Seafood** next to the stony beach or **Sin Lam Huat**, around the town square, for kampong dishes.

Singaporeans wax lyrical about the old kampong atmosphere on the island, but for years the country's rapacious developers have been slavering over it (they'd probably call it 'untapped potential') and sadly it may be only a matter of time before at least part of it surrenders.

To get to Changi Village, take a cab from the city (from $20) or take bus 2 or 29 from Tanah Merah MRT station.

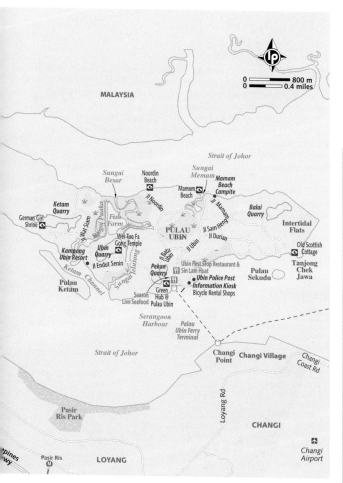

MALAYSIA

0   800 m
0   0.4 miles

Strait of Johor

Sungai Besar

Noordin Beach

Sungai Memam

Mamam Beach

Mamam Beach Campite

Balai Quarry

Ketam Quarry

German Girl Shrine

Jl Noordin

Jl Sam Heng

Intertidal Flats

Fish Farm

PULAU UBIN

Old Scottish Cottage

Wei Tuo Fa Gong Temple

Jl Ubin

Jl Sam Heng

Jl Durian

Tanjong Chek Jawa

Ubin Quarry

Jl Mamam

Pulau Sekudu

Kampong Ubin Resort

Jl Endut Senin

Jl Batu Ubin

Pulau Ketam

Pekan Quarry

Ubin First Stop Restaurant & Sin Lam Huat

Ubin Police Post
Information Kiosk
Bicycle Rental Shops

Green Hub @ Pulau Ubin

Season Live Seafood

Serangoon Harbour

Palau Ubin Ferry Terminal

Strait of Johor

Changi Point

Changi Village

Changi Coast Rd

Pasir Ris Park

Loyang Rd

CHANGI

pines
Hwy

Pasir Ris

LOYANG

Changi Airport

>HOLLAND RD & BUKIT TIMAH

Ever since the British housed their soldiers in the area, Holland Village has been a stronghold of affluent foreign residents. Today, the semicircle of bars and restaurants around Lorong Mambong and along Jl Merah Saga looks more like Sydney than Singapore.

Explore further afield and you'll find this area immediately west of the city is largely the domain of the prosperous. Dotted around the suburban streets, drawn to all the money, are small clusters of shops and restaurant-bar strips such as Greenwood Ave and Dempsey Rd, where former military barracks have been converted. In these areas you'll find the kind of neighbourhood vibe absent from much of the city centre.

Book-ending them are two of Singapore's most outstanding green spaces: the Botanic Gardens close to Orchard Rd and the Bukit Timah Nature Reserve rainforest to the west.

HOLLAND RD & BUKIT TIMAH

◉ SEE
National Orchid Garden..**1** G4
Singapore Botanic
Gardens **2** H5

⌂ SHOP
da paolo Gastronomie....**3** D4
Galerie Cho Lón **4** D4
Holland Village
Shopping Centre **5** D4
Jones the Grocer.............**6** F5
Pantry Magic **7** D4
Red House Antiques.......**8** G5
Shang Antiques...............**9** G5
Swiss Butchery **10** F1

⍾ EAT
Au Jardin Les Amis **11** G4
Greenwood Fish
Market & Bistro....**12** F1
Halia **13** G4
Holland Village
Market & Food Centre**14** D4
Island Creamery **15** G2
Original Sin..................(see 3)
PS Café.........................**16** G5
Samy's Curry
Restaurant **17** G5
Sebastien's **18** F1

▾ DRINK
Dempsey's Hut **19** G5
Hacienda **20** F5
L'Estaminet **21** F1
Red Dot Brewhouse......**22** G5
The Old Brown Shoe.....**23** F2
The Wine Company **24** H3
The Wine Network **25** F5
Wala Wala **26** D4

★ PLAY
Shermay's Cooking
School.....................(see 3)

Please see over for map

Former soldiers sharing memories at the Holland Village Market & Food Centre (p123)

SEE

BUKIT TIMAH NATURE RESERVE

☎ 6468 5736; www.nparks.gov
.sg; 177 Hindhede Dr; admission free;
🕑 8.30am-6.30pm; 🚌 170

Singapore's only surviving patch of primary rainforest has the dual honour of being its highest point – a dizzying 163m. Most walkers take the paved trail to the summit, but we suggest diving off along the North View, South View or Fern Valley paths for a distinctly out-of-Singapore experience.

MEMORIES AT OLD FORD FACTORY

☎ 6462 6724; 351 Upper Bukit Timah Rd; adult/child $3/2.50; 🕑 9am-5.30pm Mon-Fri, 9am-1.30pm Sat; 🚌 170; ♿

Site of the humiliating British surrender to the Japanese in 1942, this museum, designed to appeal to young and old alike, tells the story of the Japanese occupation – a watershed period Singapore clearly doesn't want its youth to forget.

SINGAPORE BOTANIC GARDENS

☎ 6471 7361; www.sbg.org.sg; 1 Cluny Rd; Garden admission free, Orchid Garden adult/child $5/free; 🕑 5am-midnight; 🚌 7, 105, 123; ♿

Established in 1860, this wonderful 52-hectare park retains an aura of Victorian gentility, with its swan lake, symphony stage and themed gardens (including the National

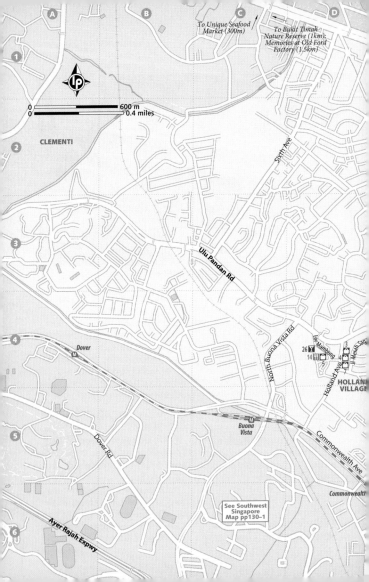

To Unique Seafood
Market (300m)

To Bukit Timah
Nature Reserve (1km);
Memories at Old Ford
Factory (1.5km)

CLEMENTI

Sixth Ave

Ulu Pandan Rd

North Buona Vista Rd

Jln Merpati

26
14

Jln Merah Saga

HOLLAND
VILLAGE

Holland Ave

Dover

Buona
Vista

Commonwealth Ave

Dover Rd

Commonwealth

See Southwest
Singapore
Map pp130-1

Ayer Rajah Expwy

600 m
0.4 miles

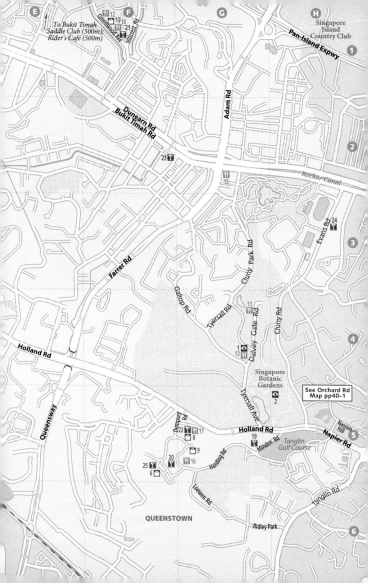

E **F** **G** **H**

To Bukit Timah
Saddle Club (500m);
Rider's Café (500m)

Greenwood Ave
12
10 6
21
Hillcrest Rd

Singapore
Island
Country
Club

Pan-Island Expwy **1**

Dunearn Rd
Bukit Timah Rd

Adam Rd

23

Rochor Canal

15

Evans Rd
24 **3**

Farrer Rd

Gallop Rd

Cluny Park Rd

Tyersall Rd

11

Dalvey Gate Rd

Cluny Rd

Holland Rd

1
13

Singapore
Botanic
Gardens
2

See Orchard Rd
Map pp40–1

Queensway

Dempsey Rd
22 17
8

Tyersall Ave

Holland Rd

19
Minden Rd

Napier Rd **5**

Nassim Hill
Tanglin
Golf
Course

Harding Rd

25 20
6 16
9

Loewen Rd

Tanglin Rd

QUEENSTOWN

Ridley Park **6**

NEIGHBOURHOODS

HOLLAND RD & BUKIT TIMAH

The Singapore Botanic Gardens (p117) offers sanctuary at the edge of busy Orchard Rd

Orchid Garden). A late-afternoon stroll along its myriad paths, followed by a drink or dinner at Halia (p123) or Au Jardin Les Amis (p123) is one of the city's most memorable experiences.

SHOP

The Holland Rd area is a great alternative to the mall madness of the city, but you'll need to do a fair bit of legwork. Dempsey Rd was an enclave of Asian antiques, art and furniture long before the current restaurant boom, while Holland Village's old mall and small shops are a good hunting ground for the unusual.

DA PAOLO GASTRONOMIA
Food
☎ 6475 1323; 43 Jl Merah Saga;
⊙ 9am-9pm; 🚌 7
Top-notch deli and the perfect place to fuel up for a shopping jaunt around Holland Village. Choose your gourmet pizza, salad, dessert, dip, bread or sandwich, then score one of the bench tables along the pavement for a picnic.

GALÉRIE CHO LÓN
Furniture, Collectables
☎ 6473 7922; 43 Jl Merah Saga;
⊙ 11am-7.30pm Mon-Fri, 11am-8.30pm Sat, noon-7pm Sun; 🚌 7

Marrying the polish of a high-end lifestyle store with the chaotic jumble of an eccentric curio shop, Cho Lón always has the ability to surprise. Among the familiar range of Asian furniture, homeware and antiques you'll find a range of books, plus things such as old-style stitched leather footballs and antique kids' bicycles. A delight.

🏠 JONES THE GROCER *Food*
☎ 6476 1512; www.jonesthegrocer .com; Block 9, Dempsey Rd; ⏰ 9.30am-11pm Tue-Sun, 9.30am-6pm Mon; 🚌 7, 67, 174, then walk; ♿
Australian posh-nosh store and bistro dedicated to high-end edibles. Wildly popular with expats, it's worth visiting for its superbly smelly cheese room, though some of the produce is ex-

A STRIKING STATISTIC
Singapore is hit by lightning on an average of 170 days every year, making it one of the lightning capitals of the world. Its year-round heat and humidity generate ideal conditions for thunderstorms, which can produce dramatic and spectacular sound-and-light displays, particularly over the sea. Remarkably, according to official figures, lightning accounts for only 0.35 deaths per million people in Singapore every year (which translates to around one person), compared with 0.6 in the US.

pensive (we noted high mark-up on items readily available in local supermarkets).

🏠 PANTRY MAGIC *Cookware*
☎ 6471 0566; www.pantry-magic.com; 43 Jl Merah Saga; ⏰ 10am-9pm Sun-Thu, 10am-10pm Fri & Sat; 🚌 7; ♿
Neatly stacked with gleaming copper, stainless steel and cast iron (there are even miniature fondue sets), this is cookware so professional it makes you want to throw a tantrum.

GETTING THERE & AROUND
> **MRT** – The area is poorly serviced by the MRT, the closest station to Holland Village being Buona Vista.
> **Bus** – Bus 174 runs from Eu Tong Sen St in Chinatown, along Orchard Rd and past the Botanic Gardens and Dempsey Rd, then turns off Holland Rd and runs the length of Bukit Timah Rd. Bus 170 runs from Little India all way the to Bukit Timah Nature Reserve. For Holland Rd, catch bus 7 from behind Orchard Rd.

🏠 RED HOUSE ANTIQUES *Antiques*
☎ 6474 6980; www.redhouseantiques .com.sg; 01-03, 26 Dempsey Rd; ⏰ 10.30am-6.30pm; 🚌 7, 67, 174; ♿
Specialist in Chinese antique furniture and restoration, Red House has been around for years and is

NEIGHBOURHOODS

HOLLAND RD & BUKIT TIMAH

HOLLAND VILLAGE SHOPPING CENTRE

This ageing, slightly run-down **building** (Map pp118–19; 211 Holland Ave) is a magnet for expats and fashionable Singaporeans and a great place for an aimless browse among the arts, handicrafts, gifts, homewares and fashion outlets. Then top it off at one of the **massage, reflexology** or **beauty salons** on level 3 for a little pampering afterwards. Most stalls open around 10am and close between 8pm and 9.30pm.

Lim's Arts & Living (Shop 01, level 2) is a virtual encyclopedia of home furnishing, from kitsch model ships to classy Middle Eastern- and Asian-style lamps and chests. **Island & Archipelago** (Shop 05, level 2) has interesting retro, beachy-style dresses, while **EMF** (Shop 24, level 2) has a large selection of secondhand books for sale, rent or trade. **Framing Angie** (Shop 02, level 3) is a classy art gallery that'll also do a great job of framing pictures. For some beautiful and unusual wooden pots and vases, take a look at **Mango Wood Crafts** (Shop 08, level 3).

On the corner outside, check out **newsstand**, which has one of the largest range of newspapers and magazines in the city. This is Singapore, so it might not be long before it's decided Holland Village needs a shiny, spanking modern identikit mall to complement its new MRT station, and this little gem is torn down.

one of the most reliable dealers in the city. There are some magnificent old pieces on display, from the smallest chair to the most enormous doors and screens.

SHANG ANTIQUES *Antiques*
☎ 6388 8838; 01-04, 16 Dempsey Rd;
🕙 11am-6.30pm; 🚌 7, 67, 174; ♿
Specialising in antique religious artefacts from Cambodia, Laos, Thailand, India and Burma, as well as reproductions, there are items in here dating back nearly 2000 years, with price tags to match.

SWISS BUTCHERY *Food*
☎ 6468 7588; 30/32 Greenwood Ave;
🕙 10am-7pm Mon-Fri, 10am-6pm Sat;
🚌 170, then walk

This is the place to come to satisfy those sausage and steak cravings. They also have a small range of sauces and a few groceries to complement the flesh frenzy.

🍴 EAT

You'd hardly know it driving through the endless residential suburbs, but there is some fantastic eating to be done in this area, concentrated around Holland Village, Dempsey Rd and Greenwood Ave. True to the style of these neighbourhoods, much of it is Western food, though if you explore a bit deeper there are plenty of cheap coffeeshops and hawker centres around as well.

AU JARDIN LES AMIS
French $$$

☎ 6466 8812; EJH Corner House, Singapore Botanic Gardens, Cluny Rd; ⏲ noon-2pm Fri, 11.30am-2pm Sun, 7-9.30pm daily; 🚌 7, 105, 123, 174, 502; ♿

It's not difficult to see why it's at the top of many food lists. Combine a dreamy botanic gardens setting with traditional French fare (pâté de fois gras and truffles) with interlopers such as tiramisu and Iranian caviar. Bookings are essential.

GREENWOOD FISH MARKET & BISTRO *Seafood* $$

☎ 6467 4950; 34 Greenwood Ave; ⏲ noon-2.30pm & 6.30-10pm; 🚌 170; ♿

Outstandingly fresh, the potential meals here are either lying on a bed of ice, or crawling around in the tank inside. Well known for its fish and chips, it also has a $1 oyster night on Tuesdays. The fishmonger stays open from 10am to 10pm.

HALIA *International* $$$

☎ 6476 6711; www.halia.com.sg; Singapore Botanic Gardens, 1 Cluny Rd; ⏲ 11am-11pm Mon-Fri, 9am-11pm Sat & Sun; 🚌 7, 105, 123, 174, 502; ♿ ♿ Ⓥ

With a location like this, nestled among the ginger plants in the botanic gardens, who needs good food? Fortunately, Halia provides that as well. Book a table on the

veranda for a perfect romantic dinner, or come for their English tea and cakes (3pm to 5pm, Monday to Saturday).

HOLLAND VILLAGE MARKET & FOOD CENTRE
Hawker Centre $

Lor Mambong; ⏲ 10am-late; 🚌 7; ♿

Despite the signboard outside telling foreigners how to navigate hawker centres and describing different dishes, few seem to venture from the pricier restaurants across the road. All the classics are here, from BBQ seafood to Katong laksa to fried *kway teow* (rice noodles).

ISLAND CREAMERY
Dessert $

☎ 6468 8859; 01-03 Serene Centre, 10 Jl Serene; ⏲ 11am-10pm; 🚌 174

Almost a religious shrine for many Singaporeans, who don't mind trekking out of their way to this tiny shop for its ice creams, sorbets and pies. Specialising in local

---

THE FOOD DETECTIVE

Disguised in a trench coat and dark glasses, flamboyant TV food detective Makansutra (aka KF Seetoh) tracks down elusive hawker stalls and food centres in search of Singapore's best cuisine. You can pick up a copy of *Makansutra's* definitive hawker-food guide at good bookshops or check out www.makansutra.com for the latest reviews.

flavours such as *teh tarik* (sweet Indian spiced tea), *cendol* (shaved iced and coconut milk dessert) and the wonderful Tiger beer sorbet, there are others devoted to its Horlicks and Nutella concoctions.

ORIGINAL SIN *Vegetarian* $$
☎ 6475 5605; 43 Jl Merah Saga; ⏲ lunch 11.30am-2.30pm Tue-Sun, dinner 6pm-10.15pm; 🚌 7; 🚻 🚶 Ⓥ
It must be pretty rare for a purely vegetarian restaurant to have so many ardent carnivorous admirers, but Original Sin's superb creations on an oft-changing menu, coupled with its long wine list and relaxed atmosphere devoid of preciousness, have won many meat-eaters over – if only temporarily.

PS CAFÉ *International* $$
☎ 6479 3343; 28b Harding Rd; ⏲ lunch 11.30am-5pm Tue-Fri, 9.30am-5pm Sat & Sun, dinner 6.30pm-midnight Mon-Thu & Sun, 6.30pm-2am Fri & Sat; 🚌 7, 123, 174; 🚶 Ⓥ
The best of the newer arrivals on Dempsey Rd, this sister restaurant of Paragon's Projectshop Café (p46) continues its reputation for fine food and good service with its Mod Oz menu. It's wildly popular, so book ahead for a seat on the veranda out the back and don't miss the desserts – banana cream and pecan pies deserve particular attention.

RIDER'S CAFÉ *Bistro* $$
☎ 6466 9819; www.riderscafe.sg; 51 Fairways Dr; ⏲ 8am-10pm Tue-Sun 🚕 taxi; 🚶 Ⓥ
There's no more peaceful spot for a meal in Singapore. Part of the Bukit Timah Saddle Club (p127), this old bungalow nestles among the paddocks with only the occasional clop of hoof (and a jazz soundtrack) breaking the silence. Go early in the morning for a perfect breakfast.

WHAT'S IN A NAME?
Singapore loves acronyms, which pepper the speech of the average citizen and confuse the hell out of visitors. (A cab driver might ask you something like: 'You wan go by which way: CTE or PIE? CTE very jam – ERP finish orredi. NDP practice finish and everyone go home watch EPL.'). The city is also fond of prosaic titles. For example, a competition was held to name Changi Airport's new budget airline terminal. The winner: Budget Terminal. Meanwhile, the committee overseeing the development of Marina Bay hired branding and image specialists to come up with a name for the area. After much deliberation and great expense, they decided on...Marina Bay. And when media and publishing giant SPH embarked on a mission to name its new paper...yes, it became the *New Paper*.

A BIT OF A BARRACKING

Dempsey Rd once felt like a real find, a hideaway of crumbling old military barracks occupied by antique shops, galleries, a couple of wine bars and the wonderful Samy's Curry Restaurant. Then Singapore's relentless developers got their mitts on it, 'rebranded' it Tanglin Village, and turned it into an 'exclusive' ghetto. The once deserted, peaceful streets are jammed with BMWs and Mercs, but don't let that fool you. In our experience, the service at much-hyped restaurants Oosh and **RedDot Brewhouse** (p126) was rotten – though the bar at the latter is worth a visit for its craft beers. However, the area still hides gems such as **PS Café** (opposite), **Hacienda** (p126) and Dempsey Rd stalwarts **The Wine Network** (p127) and **Samy's Curry** (below).

🍴 SAMY'S CURRY RESTAURANT *Indian* $$
☎ 6472 2080; Civil Service Club, Block 25, Dempsey Rd; ⏰ 11am-11pm; 🚌 7, 77, 105, 106, 123, 174; ♿ Ⓥ

For 25 years, the ceiling fans spun above the banana leaves in this leafy, open-walled, timber-shuttered colonial throwback. Then, as the area developed around them, some genius decided it was time for the timber shutters to go. The food is still magnificent, but much of the atmosphere has gone.

🍴 SEBASTIEN'S *French* $$$
☎ 6465 1980; 12 Greenwood Ave; ⏰ 6.30-10pm Tue-Sun, 9-11am & noon-2.30pm Sat & Sun; 🚌 66, 67, 174; ♿ ♿

Cosy, relaxed French bistro with a genial eponymous owner, serving up commendable classics such as *boeuf bourguignon* (pot-roast beef in red wine) and *escargot* (snails) baked in mushrooms, plus an outstanding collection of cheeses.

🍴 UNIQUE SEAFOOD MARKET *Seafood* $$
☎ Ah Yat 6883 2112, Owen 6875 1895; Grandstand, 200 Turf Club Rd; ⏰ Ah Yat 11.30am-2.30pm & 5.30-10.30pm, Owen 11.30am-10.30pm; 🚌 66, 67, 174, then walk, free Turf City shuttle from Toa Payoh Bus Interchange; ♿

When they called this unique, they weren't lying. Set in the grandstand of the old racecourse, it features a seafood market where you choose your victims from more than 50 tanks, before retiring to either the Hong Kong–style Ah Yat or pan-Asian Owen seafood restaurants. A memorable experience, particularly at weekends.

🍸 DRINK
DEMPSEY'S HUT *Pub*
☎ 6473 9609; 130E Minden Rd; ⏰ noon-1am Sun-Thu, noon-2am Fri & Sat; 🚌 7, 123, 174; ♿ ♿

Nestled among the trees, away from the Beamers and Mercs

jostling to park at Dempsey Rd, long-time resident Dempsey's Hut is refreshingly unpretentious: a no-frills outdoor pub, crumbling at the edges, with a pool table, relaxed atmosphere, relatively cheap beers and some surprisingly good food (try the New Zealand lamb).

☷ HACIENDA *Bar*
☎ 6476 2922; 13A Dempsey Rd;
☷ 5pm-2am Mon-Sat, 1pm-2am Sun;
☷ 7, 67, 123, 174; ♿
One of the best bars around the Dempsey Rd area to kick off the shoes in the garden after a long hot day, sink a few mojitos or draught beers under the trees and contemplate the evening sky – at least until the band comes on.

☷ L'ESTAMINET *Bar, Restaurant*
☎ 6465 1911; 4 Greenwood Ave;
☷ noon-midnight; ☷ 66, 67, 174
Like Oosters (p62), L'Estaminet is heavily stocked with a wide selection of Belgian beers, but the bar has a more rustic feel, more likely to be populated by shorts and T-shirts than shirts and trousers. It also serves up some superb wood-fired pizzas. Head to Sebastien's (p125) for dessert afterwards.

☷ RED DOT BREWHOUSE *Microbrewery*
☎ 6475 0500; 25A Dempsey Rd;
☷ noon-11pm Sun-Thu, noon-1am Fri & Sat; ☷ 7, 67, 123, 174
The service at the restaurant here was shocking, which is a shame,

WORTH THE TRIP
Not as manic as the track in Hong Kong, but nevertheless the **Singapore Turf Club** (☎ 6879 1000; www.turfclub.com.sg; 1 Turf Club Ave; air-con/nonair-con $7/3, private lounge $20; Ⓜ Kranji; ♿) is a great day out and a rare chance to see Singaporeans getting worked up.

There is a choice of seating in the four-storey grandstand: an open nonair-con area, an air-con area and the @Hibiscus lounge – though there's a strict dress code in there and anyone wearing jeans, open shoes or missing a collar at the neck will not be allowed in. Women get off lighter, but still require closed shoes.

For the best atmosphere, head for the sweaty cheap seats to cheer on your nag among the serious punters and dodgy characters.

All betting is, you guessed it, government controlled and the minimum bet is $5. Odds are deceptive: 5-1 odds, for example, means you win $5 for every $5 unit you bet, not $5 for every dollar, as in other places.

Races take place on Wednesday and Friday evenings, starting at 6.30pm, and on Saturdays and Sundays, starting at 1.45pm. Check the website for the calendar.

Massive sums of money pass through the windows on race days, which makes you wonder why there was such a fuss about the casinos. The Turf Club is right next to Kranji MRT station.

because this microbrewery is the product of one Singaporean man's passion for beer – and his beers are pretty damn good. So go along and plonk yourself at the bar, where the staff can't ignore you, or take 40 minutes to bring your drinks.

▼ THE OLD BROWN SHOE *Pub*

☎ 6468 4626; 619F Bukit Timah Rd; ☾ 4pm-midnight Mon-Fri, 4pm-1am Sat & Sun; 🚌 66, 67, 174; ♿

Classic British-style pub that gets especially jammed on Wednesday nights for its pub quiz, which draws competitive types from far outside the pub's usual Bukit Timah catchment area.

▼ THE WINE COMPANY *Wine Bar*

☎ 6732 6698; Evans Lodge, 26 Evans Rd; ☾ noon-midnight Mon-Thu, noon-1am Fri & Sat, 11am-11pm Sun; 🚌 66, 67, 174

Casual, relaxed, unstuffy wine bar in a quiet location opposite the National University of Singapore sports grounds. Places particular emphasis on offering 'affordable' wines, principally from South Africa.

▼ THE WINE NETWORK *Wine Bar*

☎ 6479 2280; Block 13, Dempsey Rd; ☾ 11am-midnight Sun-Thu, 11am-1am Fri & Sat; 🚌 7, 123, 174; ♿

An old favourite of Dempsey Rd aficionados whose patronage

predates the area's recent yup-pification. Sit and pine for the old days over a large wine list in the bare brick, barrel-scented interior, or on the peaceful wooden deck outside. Order some cheese plat-ters to ward off hunger before dinner at PS Café (p124) or Samy's Curry (p125).

▼ WALA WALA *Café, Bar*

☎ 6462 4288; 31 Lor Mambong; ☾ 4pm-1am Mon-Thu, 3pm-2am Fri & Sat, 3pm-1am Sun; 🚌 7

Large, raucous but friendly, Wala Wala has been a long-standing favourite with the young expat crowd for its breezy vibe and its live-music bar upstairs, where the focus is on danceable, singable, air-punchable tunes.

★ PLAY

⬛ BUKIT TIMAH SADDLE CLUB

☎ 6466 2782; www.btsc.org.sg; 51 Fairways Dr; 🚌 taxi

The good news: this feels a million miles from Singapore, tucked into a large area of countryside, with 100 stables, around 30 horses, three arenas, several trails and 10 paddocks. It has a fantastic bistro too, in the shape of the Rider's Café (p124). The bad news: the cheapest way you'll get a ride is to buy a one-month trial member-ship for $460, which includes four lessons.

>SOUTHWEST SINGAPORE

Bisected by the roaring, truck-laden Ayer Rajah Expressway and home to Singapore's mighty container terminals and industrial parks, this corner of the city is often overlooked by visitors, who pass through only to take the cable car between Mt Faber and Sentosa (p96).

But there is another side to the area. Hidden among all the economic activity are two of the country's best urban retreats – Kent Ridge Park and Labrador Nature Reserve – which, despite their absorbing historical sites and fantastic views, are virtually deserted during the week.

The Sentosa gateway area has had a massive injection of life with the opening of the vast waterfront Vivocity shopping and entertainment mall and, across the road, the brilliantly converted St James Power Station, which houses one of the city's most popular bar complexes.

SOUTHWEST SINGAPORE

👁 SEE
Kent Ridge Park..............1 C3
Labrador Secret
    Tunnels....................2 E6
Mt Faber Park 3 G5
Reflections at Bukit
    Chandu....................4 C4

🛍 SHOP
Vivocity 5 H6

🍴 EAT
Faber Hill Bistro..............6 G5
Imperial Herbal
    Restaurant ....(see 5)
Peramakan 7 F5
The Olive.......................8 E6
Villa Bali 9 E4

🍸 DRINK
Altivo & Glass Bar........(see 6)
Colbar 10 D2

Privé 11 F6
St James Power
    Station...................12 H6

⭐ PLAY
Villa Raintree Resort &
    Spa.........................13 E6

Please see over for map

SEE

KENT RIDGE PARK
Vigilante Dr; ⏰ 24hr; 🚌 200, then walk
Commanding sweeping views over the port, outer islands and Indonesia beyond, it's astonishing that Kent Ridge Park is so deserted. But that's also what makes it one of the best urban escapes in Singapore, because you have kilometres of paths and the treetop boardwalk pretty much to yourself. Check out Reflections at Bukit Chandu (p132) while you're there.

LABRADOR NATURE RESERVE
Labrador Villa Rd; ⏰ 24hr; Ⓜ HarbourFront, then bus 408 (Sat & Sun), taxi
Combining historical sites, long trails through forest rich in bird life, great views from Singapore's only sea cliffs and a beachfront park, Labrador Park is well worth an afternoon. Examine the old British guns, hike through the jungle, visit the Secret Tunnels (below) and the pillbox on the beach, then have a picnic, or a fancy meal at The Olive (p133) followed by a spa treatment at Villa Raintree (p135).

LABRADOR SECRET TUNNELS
☎ 6339 6833; Labrador Villa Rd, Labrador Nature Reserve; adult/child $8/5; ⏰ 10am-7pm; Ⓜ HarbourFront, then bus 408 (Sat & Sun), taxi

> **GETTING THERE & AROUND**
> > **Bus** – 408 from HarbourFront MRT runs along the main artery through the area.

A series of storage and armament bunkers built by the British in the 1880s that incredibly remained undiscovered for 50 years after WWII, until they were unearthed when work began on turning Labrador into a nature reserve. Small, but fascinating, there are displays of artefacts left behind when the British abandoned the tunnels in 1942, as well as the buckled and caved-in walls from a direct hit from a Japanese bomb.

MT FABER PARK
☎ 6377 9688; www.mountfaber.com; 109 Mt Faber Rd; Ⓜ HarbourFront, then cable car, bus 409 (Sat & Sun), or walk
Standing 166m above the south fringe of the city, the Pulau Brani port and HarbourFront, Mt Faber's steeply terraced trails wind through humming forest, past strategically positioned viewpoints. Run by a leisure group, it's a lot busier and more commercial than Kent Ridge or Labrador parks, but it also boasts bars with some of best views in the city. The exhilarating **cable car** (adult/child return $11.90/6.50; ⏰ 8.30pm-11pm) is the best way to get to and from the hill.

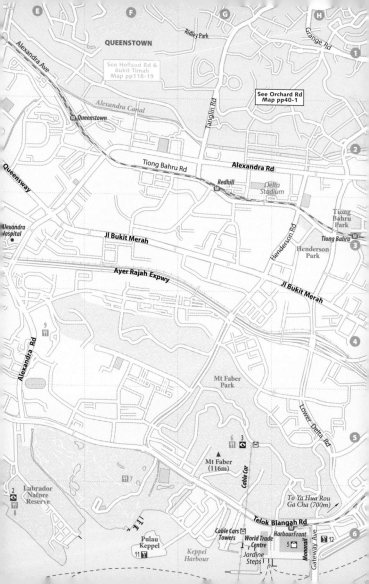

QUEENSTOWN

E
F
G
H

1

Grange Rd

Ridley Park

Alexandra Ave

See Holland Rd &
Bukit Timah
Map pp118–19

Tanglin Rd

See Orchard Rd
Map pp40–1

Alexandra Canal

M Queenstown

2

Tiong Bahru Rd
Alexandra Rd

Queensway

Redhill

Delta
Stadium

Henderson Rd

Tiong
Bahru
Park

Alexandra
Hospital

Jl Bukit Merah

Tiong Bahru M
3

Henderson
Park

Ayer Rajah Expwy

Jl Bukit Merah

Alexandra Rd

9

4

Mt Faber
Park

Lower Delta Rd

5

6 3

Mt Faber
(116m)

Cable Car

2

7

Labrador
Nature
Reserve

8

11

Pulau
Keppel

Telok Blangah Rd

To Ya Hua Rou
Ga Cha (700m)

Cable Cars
Towers

World Trade
Centre

5

HarbourFront

12

Monorail

Gateway Ave

6

Keppel
Harbour

Jardine
Steps

⊙ REFLECTIONS AT BUKIT CHANDU

☎ 6375 2510; www.s1942.org.sg; 31K Pepys Rd; adult/child $2/1; ☻ 9am-5pm Tue-Sun; 🚌 10, 30, 143; ♿

Commemorating the last stand of the Malay Regiment against the Japanese in 1942, and an ode to the old kampong days that have vanished from Singapore. Combines first-hand accounts, artefacts such as old guns and helmets, films and dramatisations to describe the tragic and brutal battle that almost wiped the regiment out.

🍴 EAT

🍴 FABER HILL BISTRO
Western $$

☎ 6377 9688; 101 Mt Faber Rd; ☻ 9am-1am Sun-Tue, 9am-2am Wed-Sat; Ⓜ HarbourFront, then cable car, bus 409 Sat & Sun, or walk; ♿ 🚼

The high canopy makes it feel a little like you're inside a wedding marquee, but with views like this from Mt Faber Hill you'll only be looking outwards. The steaks and pastas are just good enough to complement the twinkling skyline.

🍴 IMPERIAL HERBAL RESTAURANT Chinese $$

☎ 6337 0491; 03-08, Lobby G, Vivocity; ☻ 11.30am-2.30pm & 6-10pm; Ⓜ HarbourFront; ♿ Ⓥ

Feeling a little under? Have your pulse checked, tongue examined and physical ailments remedied and your body rebalanced with a precise prescription of herbal soups, double-boiled chickens and other more esoteric ingredients.

🍴 PERAMAKAN Peranakan $$

☎ 6375 5563; L3 Keppel Club, 10 Bukit Chermin Rd; ☻ 11.30am-3pm & 6-10pm; Ⓜ HarbourFront, then bus 93

Run by a genial couple of cooking enthusiasts, this paragon of

---

WORTH THE TRIP

Staggeringly large, the waterfront **Vivocity** (☎ 6377 6860; 1 HarbourFront Walk; ☻ 10am-10pm; Ⓜ HarbourFront; ♿) megamall is Singapore's largest, and offers a viable alternative to pavement pounding on Orchard Rd, though its broad, squat design (by Japanese architect Toyo Ito) means there's still a prodigious amount of walking to do. There are dozens of ubiquitous fashion chains such as **Diesel**, **Hang Ten** and **Esprit** (and locals such as **M)phosis**) as well as smaller boutiques. Electronics giants such as **Denki** and **Challenger** also have a heavy presence. The excellent **Page One** bookshop is a rival to Kinokuniya in Orchard Rd, while the **Golden Village** cineplex is also Singapore's largest, with luxury Gold Class, GVMax and Cinema Europa cinemas. At night the waterfront side resembles a lower key version of Sydney's Darling Harbour, with top-end restaurants and a few lounge bars catching the evening breeze.

homestyle Baba-Nonya cuisine has migrated from its spiritual Joo Chiat home, but the classics such as *sambal* (spicy shrimp paste) squid and *rendang* (spicy coconut curry) remain as good as ever.

THE OLIVE *Italian* $$$
☎ 6479 2989; Labrador Villa Rd, Labrador Park; ⏰ noon-11pm Mon-Sat, 9am-11pm Sun; Ⓜ HarbourFront, then bus 408 (Sat & Sun), taxi; ♿ ⛲ Ⓥ
Tucked away on a hill inside thickly forested Labrador Park, The Olive cries out for a romantic occasion, with the city lights twinkling through the trees over some fine pasta. Worth the effort to get there.

YA HUA ROU GU CHA
Chinese $
☎ 6222 9610; 7 Keppel Rd, PSA Tanjong Pagar Complex; ⏰ 7am-3pm Tue-Sun; Ⓜ Tanjong Pagar
There's no such thing as 'location, location, location' when it comes to hawker food. Singaporeans would crawl through a sewage pipe if there were a good meal at the end of it, so the positioning of this famous *bak kut teh* (pork-rib soup) joint next to the port and beside an expressway doesn't stop the multitudes from coming to sip peppery broth and gnaw on bones.

KAMPONG DAYS
Fifty years ago the view from Mt Faber, Kent Ridge and Labrador Parks would have been vastly different. Until the 1950s, most Singaporeans lived in single-storey homes in their kampong (traditional Malay village) on these hills – and countless other places – but population pressures and land scarcity saw them forced out. Singaporeans remain sentimental about the kampong but, as an old Malay veteran says in the documentary at **Reflections at Bukit Chandu** (opposite), 90% of them now live in 'comfortable HDB flats'. (Of course, he wasn't told to say they are 'comfortable'!)

🍸 DRINK

ALTIVO & GLASS BAR *Bar*
☎ 6377 9688; 109 Mt Faber Rd; ⏰ 9am-1am Sun-Tue, 9am-3am Wed-Sat; Ⓜ HarbourFront, then cable car, bus 409 (Sat & Sun), or walk; ♿
Part of the small complex atop Mt Faber Hill that sucks in the cable car and spits it out towards Sentosa, the Altivo outdoor lounge and impossibly hip indoor Glass Bar are both magical spots to watch dusk slide into night over the sea below.

🍸 COLBAR *Bar, Café*
☎ 6779 4859; 9A Whitchurch Rd; ⏰ 11am-10pm Tue-Sun; 🚌 100, 123, 147, then walk; ♿
Something of an institution, Colbar attracts a loyal crowd of weekend

regulars drawn to the bare-bones décor, friendly service, wanton Sunday drunkenness and hangover-friendly fry-ups and curries.

▼ PRIVÉ Bar, Restaurant

☎ 6766 0777; Keppel Bay Dr; ⏰ noon-1am Sun-Thu, noon-2am Fri & Sat; Ⓜ HarbourFront, then taxi; ♿

Located on an island in the middle of Keppel Harbour, with the city on one side and Sentosa on the other, you couldn't ask for a better location for drinks or brunch. Attracts an affluent crowd. There are guest DJs and occasional live music. The attached Australian-style restaurant is worth staying for.

▼ VILLA BALI Bar, Restaurant

☎ 9750 2140; www.littlebali.com; 9A Lock Rd, Gillman Village; ⏰ 4pm-1am

ST JAMES POWER STATION

New poster boy of Singapore's night scene, St James (☎ 6270 7676; www.stjamespowerstation.com; 3 Sentosa Gateway; men/women $12/10, Wed men $20; Ⓜ HarbourFront; ♿) is quite an achievement. Converting a 1920s coal-fired power station into an entertainment complex took both huge amounts of money and a fair scoopful of design talent. All the bars and clubs are interconnected, so one cover charge gets access to all of them. Several bars – the Bellini Room, Gallery Bar, Lobby Bar and Peppermint Park – have no cover charge at all. Minimum age is 18 for women and 23 for men at all except Powerhouse, where the age is 18 for both.

> **Bellini Room** (⏰ 8pm-3am Mon-Thu, 8pm-4am Fri & Sat) Cool, stylish jazz and swing bar lit in deep red and blue, with a live band doing sets throughout the night. Great fun.

> **Dragonfly** (⏰ 6pm-6am) Hugely popular Cantopop and Mandopop club, with live bands (featuring regulation sexily clad girls and spiky-haired boys) and a curious PVC pipe ceiling design. Expect to be the only foreigner in here.

> **Gallery Bar** (⏰ 8pm-3am Mon-Thu, 8pm-4am Fri & Sat) Ingeniously designed glass-walled bar offering views into the four main clubs but shielded from the noise of each. Great spot to retreat, relax and decide where to go next.

> **Momo** (⏰ 6pm-6am) Karaoke bar with 10 private rooms, done out like a horror-movie French bordello.

> **Movida** (⏰ 6pm-3am) Decked out like a '70s disco, this Latin dance club features an excellent, eye-catching, thoroughly danceable band from Paraguay. The best of the lot.

> **Peppermint Park** (⏰ 6pm-3am Mon-Thu, 6pm-4am Fri & Sat) Outdoor chill-out area with a bar, large day beds and swing seats.

> **Powerhouse** (⏰ 8pm-4am Wed, Fri & Sat) Industrial design and a huge dance space aimed at a younger crowd.

> **The Boiler Room** (⏰ 8.45pm-3am Mon-Sat) Straight-up, no frills rock and pop club, with a Filipino band performing Western hits to a largely table-bound audience.

The Bellini Room is one of eight themed rooms at the ultrahip St James Power Station

Mon-Thu, 4pm-2am Fri & Sat, 9.30am-3pm, 4pm-1am Sun; 🚌 57, 195; ♿
The highlight of this relaxed garden bar is the private wooden platforms, where you can recline back on some cushions, sink a few drinks and some decent Indian snacks.

⭐ PLAY

⭐ CLIMB ADVENTURE
☎ 6220 3305; www.climbadventure.com; 02-01, 12 West Coast Walk; per day $10, beginner's workshop $25; 🕙 10am-10pm Tue-Fri, 10am-6pm Sat & Sun; Ⓜ Clementi, then taxi
Serious climbing gym equipped with more than 40 'lanes'. There

are lanes catering to various levels of ability, from kid beginners to fingertip danglers.

⭐ VILLA RAINTREE RESORT & SPA
☎ 6532 1155; www.villaraintree.com; 30 Labrador Rd, Labrador Nature Reserve; Ⓜ HarbourFront, then bus 408 Sat & Sun, taxi; ♿
Singapore has more spas than it knows what to do with, but few can boast views like this converted colonial bungalow overlooking the Strait of Singapore. Costs from $50, for a basic back and shoulder massage, to $310, for some scientific facial magic.

>JURONG

It's hard to decide whether placing a whole gamut of child-friendly attractions in a working-class industrial suburb was inspired or bizarre, but nonetheless there they are. The world-class Jurong Bird Park, Science Centre, indoor snow slope and Imax cinema can keep the little ones (and yourself) occupied for a couple of days, but it's a fair hike out from the city centre and, once you're there, there isn't a good deal else in the way of shops or restaurants.

However, one saving grace is the superb Hilltop Japanese Restaurant, a short walk up from the Jurong Bird Park, plus a half-decent Peranakan joint in the Science Centre.

JURONG

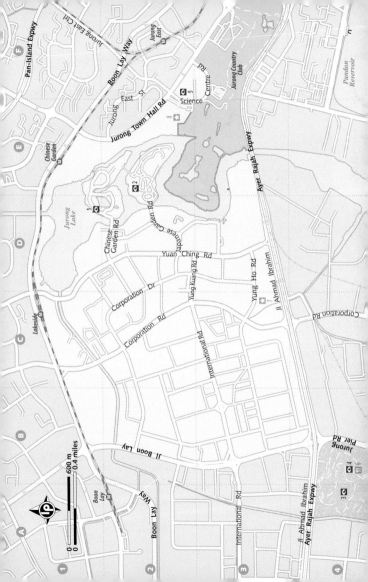

NEIGHBOURHOODS

JURONG

Cockatoo (and a trainer) providing entertainment at the Jurong Bird Park

SEE

CHINESE & JAPANESE GARDENS

☎ 6261 3632; 1 Chinese Garden Rd; 🕐 6am-11pm; Ⓜ Chinese Garden; 🛗

A thoroughly pleasant recreation of a classical Chinese garden, set against a backdrop of public housing, this is probably best combined with a trip to the Jurong Bird Park and/or Science Centre. The highlight is the truly outstanding bonsai collection (the centrepiece tree is 300 years old!). The neighbouring Japanese Garden is rather sparse and hardly worth the walk.

JURONG BIRD PARK

☎ 6265 0022; www.birdpark.com .sg; 2 Jurong Hill; adult/child $18/9, panorail adult/child $4/2; 🕐 9am-6pm; Ⓜ Boon Lay, then bus 194, 251; 🛗

Boasting one of the largest bird collections in the world, the Jurong Bird Park is a mixed bag of enthralling open-concept aviaries and depressing little cages (the latter are slowly being fazed out, hopefully). Be sure not to miss the Waterfall Aviary (which has the largest man-made falls on earth), the African Wetlands and the Lori Loft, and the fantastic Birds of Prey show.

Andrew Duffy
Lecturer, Nanyang Technological University (and father of three)

Best places to take the kids? We go to Sentosa (p96) at least once a month because there's always something new to do. The Jacob Ballas Children's Garden is a strange wonderland. Otherwise we follow activities attached to festivals, like Chinese Garden for the Lantern Festival, or Little India for Deepavali and Thaipusam. **And on a rainy day?** The Science Centre (p140) has lots of hands-on activities to keep them entertained, plus travelling exhibitions. **Favourite spot to escape to?** Kent Ridge Park (p129). There are views out to sea and a fresh breeze. Best of all, there are never more than a dozen people there. **If you had one day left in Singapore, where would you eat and drink?** *Roti prata* (fried flat bread) and *teh tarik* (pulled tea) at Telok Blangah Rise, *sambal* (spicy shrimp paste) stingray at East Coast Lagoon Food Village for lunch, and dinner at Gayatri on Race Course Rd, followed by a drink at Parkview Sq, where a girl on a trapeze gets your bottle from a 10m-high wine rack.

People experimenting with interactive displays at Singapore Science Centre

 JURONG LOOKOUT TOWER

Jurong Hill; Ⓜ Jurong East, then bus 194, 251

A curious relic of the 1970s (as if you couldn't tell), this viewing tower boasts a stained glass ceiling and a futuristic night-time view over the lights and flaming stacks of the Jurong Island industrial zone. Take a hike up after the Jurong Bird Park (p138) and eat at Hilltop Japanese Restaurant (opposite) in the basement afterwards.

SINGAPORE SCIENCE CENTRE

☎ 6425 2500; www.science.edu.sg; 15 Science Centre Rd; adult/child $6/3, with Snow City $15/13, with Imax movie $12.80/6.40; ⏱ 10am-6pm Tue-Sun, Mon during school holidays; Ⓜ Jurong East; ♿

The kids might moan when they hear the unimaginative name of this attraction, but once unleashed inside they'll probably forget science is boring. A huge collection of interactive exhibits, covering subjects such as outer space, the human body and visual illusions, plus frequent travelling exhibitions, can swallow up an entire day, especially if coupled with Snow City and the Omni theatre which screens Imax films.

🍴 EAT

🍴 HILLTOP JAPANESE RESTAURANT *Japanese* $$

☎ 6266 3522; 2 Jurong Hill; 🕙 11.30am-10.30pm; Ⓜ Jurong East, then bus 194, 251; ♿

As if finding a Japanese restaurant here isn't strange enough, it turns out to be a Japanese-Indonesian restaurant to boot. Most diners come for the excellent teppanyaki, a few Asahis and a climb up the observation tower afterwards, though you can get your *nasi goreng* (fried rice) and *gado gado* (vegetable salad with peanut sauce) too.

⭐ PLAY

⭐ KART WORLD *Kart Racing*

☎ 6266 2555; www.kartworld.com.sg; Yung Ho Rd; adult/child per 10min $40/28; 🕙 11am-10pm; Ⓜ Jurong East, then bus 98M

With prices like this, you know Kart World must be serious about racing. The 700m track is challenging and the karts are pretty quick. It works out to be better value for money if you can get a decent-sized

WORTH THE TRIP

The **Sungei Buloh Wetland Reserve** (☎ 6794 1401; www.sbwr.org.sg; 301 Neo Tiew Crescent; Mon-Fri admission free, adult/child Sat, Sun, public & school holidays $1/0.50; 🕙 7.30am-7pm Mon-Sat, 7am-7pm Sun; Ⓜ Kranji, then bus 925) is a 87-hectare nature reserve in far northwest Singapore overlooking the Strait of Johor, and home to 140 species of birds. It's been declared a nature reserve and recognised as a sanctuary of international importance as part of the East Asia Flyway.

The best time for viewing birds is before 10am, and if you go on a weekday the reserve is blissfully serene. Be prepared for encounters with several monitor lizards, some of them unnervingly large, and sightings of playful otter families hunting fish. There are also, apparently, saltwater crocodiles in the area, though sightings (thankfully) seem to be rare.

From the visitors centre trails lead around ponds and mangroves to small hides decked out with signboards that'll help you identify the different species. There's also a three-storey aerie. Allow three hours to do the reserve justice.

Free guided tours begin at 9.30am and 3.30pm on Saturdays. On other days, tours have to be prebooked and cost $50 per group. Audiovisual shows on the park's flora and fauna are held at 9am, 11am, 1pm, 3pm and 5pm (hourly between 9am and 5pm on Sunday).

On weekdays, the bus stops at the end of Neo Tiew Crescent, a 10-minute walk from the park. On Sundays, the bus goes right to the park entrance.

BEERS BY THE BOWSPRIT

As far away as it's possible to get from the city, **Raffles Marina** (☎ 6861 8000; www.rafflesmarina.com.sg; 10 Tuas West Dr; Ⓜ Boon Lay, then bus 192, 193) is a surreal world of clanging halyards, cawing birds and salty stories out in the industrial wastelands of Singapore's far west. Temporary home to travelling yachties and a few boat-dwelling residents, it's a great place to sit at sunset over dinner with a few beers – even better if you have a few seaman's tales to share. Have a dock-side dinner at **Marina Bistro** (☎ 6869 2299; ⏱ 8am-10pm), then a beer at the **Discovery Pub** (☎ 6869 2277; ⏱ noon-midnight). There's also a bowling alley and a billiard room.

group together and stage a tournament, which costs $1300 per hour.

⭐ **SNOW CITY** *Playground*
☎ 6560 2306; www.snowcity.com.sg; adult/child $15/13; ⏱ 9.45am-5.15pm Tue-Sun; Ⓜ Jurong East

Recent arrivals from winter climates might fail to see the appeal here, but throwing yourself down a snow-covered 70m slope on a huge inner tube in -5°C temperatures until you lose all feeling in your extremities is a big draw if you live most of your life in 90% humidity. Kids will defintely love it while adults can sneak off to the bar. Sessions last an hour and tickets get you entry into the Singapore Science Centre (p140) next door.

>WALKING TOURS

The view of Fullerton Hotel across the Singapore River

COLONIAL NIGHT WALK

There are three very good reasons to explore the Colonial District at night: you don't get baked in the sun, the traffic is significantly lighter and the buildings are beautifully lit.

Start around 7pm, taking exit B from **Dhoby Ghaut MRT (1)**. Walk left along Penang Rd and where the road bends to the left, nip across and climb the stairs next to the Fort Canning Tunnel exit. Down Fort Canning Rd on the

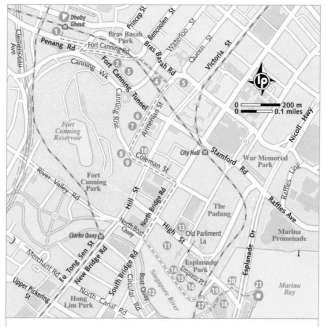

distance 3.5km **duration** 50min ▶ **start** Ⓜ Dhoby Ghaut ⬤ **end** Boat Quay

right, the **Wesley Methodist Church (2)** dates back to 1908 (the original stained-glass windows were recovered from the wreckage of the Japanese retreat).

Next up is the magnificent **National Museum of Singapore (3**; p70) – add 10 minutes for a wander through the building, saving a visit for later.

A stroll between the **Singapore Management University (4)** buildings provides a modern counterpoint to the area's Victorian structures. Turn right – noting the **Church of the Good Shepherd (5)** to the left – cross Stamford Rd into dimly lit Armenian St, past the **Substation (6**; p80) theatre (time for a drink around the back?) and the **Peranakan Museum (7**; p70).

Head left into Coleman St and past the stately **Philatelic Museum (8)**, **Masonic Hall (9)** and, hidden among the trees to the left, the **Armenian Church (10)**.

Cross Hill St, continue down Coleman St, then turn right into North Bridge Rd. After the marble **Parliament (11)** emerges to the left, you're rewarded with a wonderful view of the river, the rumbling bumboats and lights of **Boat Quay (12)**, dwarfed by the thicket of skyscrapers in the financial district.

Look back at the **Supreme Court (13)**, then descend the steps to the promenade. Pass the **statue of Sir Stamford Raffles (14)**, marking the spot he first landed in Singapore, **Indochine (15)** and the **Asian Civilisations Museum (16**; p67), before crossing **Cavenagh Bridge (17)** – check out the cats to the right of the bridge. Turn left along the river, past the **Fullerton Hotel (18)** diners, cross the **Anderson Bridge (19)**, then dive down to the left of the **Waterboat House (20)** and walk under the Esplanade Drive bridge (past the unexpected Starbucks underneath!) to the **Merlion Park (21)** for a great view of the Esplanade theatres, Suntec City, Singapore Flyer and (if it's built by then) the Marina Bay Sands.

Double back, retrace your steps to Boat Quay and reward yourself with a drink at the Archipelago (p75) microbrewery on Circular Rd.

Take a break from the manic city at idyllic Fort Canning Park (p39)

SINGAPORE NATURE TRAIL

Begin at **MacRitchie Reservoir Park (1)** – carrying lots of water – then follow the path around the right side of the reservoir until you reach a fork. Take the boardwalk to the left, keeping an eye out for macaques (keep any food hidden, or they can get aggressive), monitor lizards, flying lemurs and terrapins.

Follow the water's edge until the boardwalk ends and connects you to the **MacRitchie Nature Trail (2)** track. After 2km you hit a paved road at the **Island Country Club (3)**.

Turn left along the road, then take the next road left, which ends at the Kallang Service Reservoir. Follow the signs to the **Treetop Walk (4)**, cross the bridge, looking out for sunbathing snakes, then follow the boardwalk through the forest.

Spot primates at the MacRitchie Reservoir Park

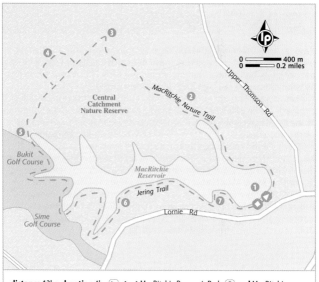

distance 12km **duration** 4hr ▶ **start** MacRitchie Reservoir Park ◉ **end** MacRitchie Reservoir Park

Turn right onto the Sime Track until you reach the **Jelutong Tower (5)** – climb for a view.

Follow the track until you reach a sign for the Jering Trail, which hugs the edge of the reservoir. Look out for a mysterious **Chinese tombstone (6)** – no-one knows who is buried there.

Finally, cross the strange **zigzag bridge (7)** and climb the small hill for a rewarding drink at the food centre back where you started.

WALKING TOURS

CHINATOWN

Emerge from **Chinatown MRT (1)** on Pagoda St and battle through the stalls to Trengganu St, where you turn right. After crossing Temple St, look up at the rickety balustrade running around the early 20th-century building to your left. Grab a sausage from **Erich's Wuerstelstand (2**; p57-8) and turn left down Sago St until you reach South Bridge Rd. Turn right, admiring the **Buddha Tooth Relic Temple(3**; p51), then cross the street and head to the **Maxwell Rd Hawker Centre (4**; p59). Turn left up Kadayanallur St, passing the gothic **Scarlet Hotel (5)**, then follow the road past the old clan headquarters and renovated shophouses to Ann Siang Hill. Walk up the hill, down the iron spiral staircase to your left, then turn right, descending to Amoy St, peeking in at the **Siang Cho Keong Temple (6)**. Turn left into Telok Ayer St, passing the **Al-Abrar Mosque (7)** before reaching the beautiful **Thian Hock Keng Temple (8**; p54). Continue on past **Telok Ayer Garden (9)** and the restored **Nagore Durgha Shrine (10)**, traverse Cross St, then duck through the ancient doorway of the **Fuk Tak Ch'i Museum (11)** emerging, surreally, out the back door into the air-conditioned comfort of Far East Sq.

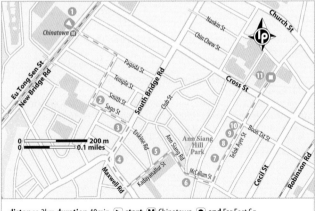

distance 2km **duration** 40min ▶ **start** Ⓜ Chinatown ● **end** Far East Sq

>THE NEW SINGAPORE

Ultramodern and efficient Dhoby Ghaut MRT Station

THE NEW SINGAPORE

Change is hardly new to Singapore – the island has been in a near constant state of flux since it was founded, but today's city is undergoing the kind of social and physical transition it hasn't seen since the manic construction boom of the '60s and '70s. The closed, tightly controlled society for which it became famous is looking increasingly fragile. Though the government's ruthless grip on political power is unlikely to be loosened, Singapore simply cannot survive by looking inwards, so it is being forced to try and shed the insular parochialism of old and remake itself in the image of the cosmopolitan, freewheeling metropolises around the world it aspires to emulate.

The principal reasons are, of course, economic. Manufacturing – once the country's engine room – is migrating to cheaper climes, so Singapore is having to reinvent itself fast as a hub for everything from financial services to aviation to biomedical engineering to tourism, conventions, entertainment and sports. And to support this globalised economic base, it needs to import people – another two million of them, in the government's estimation.

It's a change that promises to utterly transform the city and, possibly, the ever-widening income gap will mean many people, most of them Singaporeans, are left behind. It will be intriguing to see what effect this has on the city's rock-hard social stability.

Dempsey Rd (p125) is home to flashy cars and posh restaurants

INTEGRATED RESORTS

Singapore is accustomed to large-scale construction projects, but few have generated the kind of interest now focused on its two casinos (known by the fluffy official moniker of 'integrated resorts'). When complete in 2009 and 2010, these two vast and expensive projects at **Marina Bay** (www.marinabaysands.com) and on **Sentosa Island** (www.resortsworldatsentosa.com) will feature extravagant attractions such as a Universal Studios theme park, the world's largest aquarium, museums, massive hotels and, of course, casinos.

Primarily targeted at affluent tourists and the high-rolling super-rich, the resorts form the keystone of the city's bid to plant its flag more aggressively on the world tourism map and become a destination in its own right, rather than a place people pass through on their way to somewhere else. (A senior analyst at a global financial house suggested the projects were money-laundering engines for China's super-rich – and promptly lost his job after his comments were leaked!)

The decision to build the casinos, coming from a country well-known for its strict official morals, raised a few eyebrows at home and abroad, and for once there was vocal domestic opposition from certain quarters, principally concerned about the potential effect of casinos and their attendant ills of prostitution and crime on Singapore's carefully nurtured social order (though in fact, thousands of Singaporeans already go on 'gambling cruises' and pile across to Batam and Genting Highlands for betting orgies).

In response, the resort owners – the Sands (from the US) and Genting (from Malaysia) – have pledged to impose entrance fees for Singaporeans using the casinos, a move designed to discourage low-income locals from gambling, while counselling services for problem gamblers have been loudly trumpeted as a deterrent measure.

ENTERTAINMENT

Once derided as Singabore, the Lion City has taken a serious look at the subject of fun (to paraphrase one government minister) and seen that it is good. The results of a nightlife makeover have been mixed, but largely successful, and Singapore has earned itself a solid regional reputation for partying.

Zouk (p81), for so long the city's flagship nightclub, now has serious competition in the shape of the Ministry of Sound (p80), and entertainment precincts such as Clarke Quay and the converted St James Power Station (p134) are booming. Periodic beach parties on Sentosa have also attracted people from around the region, though there have been rumours they will come to an end.

The atmosphere is boozy, hedonistic and participants are often skimpily dressed, and the official message (rendered slightly redundant by virtue of its officialdom) is that Singapore is Cool, Hip and Happening.

The farcical battles of the past, which once saw the legality of bar-top dancing debated at the highest political levels, have not been entirely consigned to history however. The Nation and SnowBall gay parties were shut down, after the government said they were contributing to a rise in HIV infections (though thousands of illegal prostitutes at Orchard Towers and in Geylang operate with limited harassment).

A branch of the French Crazy Horse raunchy naked revue show, which opened at Clarke Quay to much fanfare and media flutter, also failed, largely because of official restrictions on advertising and public displays of flesh.

SPORTS

There is scarcely a field of human endeavour for which Singapore does not want to make itself a 'hub', and sports is no exception. The city's aggressive, almost manic, attempts to sell itself to the world scored a massive boost when it was picked to host a Formula 1 (F1) race in September 2008 (see www.singaporegp.sg), sending the local media spin-machine into overdrive. Not only that, it won approval to host the first ever F1 night race, no doubt to the vast relief of the drivers and spectators who get to avoid the stifling heat of the day. (The F1 bid was also one in the eye for long-time Grand Prix host Malaysia, and doubtless pleased Singapore no end!)

Whether the F1 race will become a regular event remains to be seen, but it brought to a close Singapore's longstanding, Lee Kuan Yew–imposed opposition to motorsport. There's now talk of building a new motorsports hub (what else?) and bringing other racing events to the city.

Singapore's other sporting endeavours include a successful bid to host the first Youth Olympics in 2010. Hand in hand with that bid is the development of a modern sports complex on the site of the old and somewhat embarrassingly decrepit National Stadium in Kallang, which was demolished in 2007. The new complex is scheduled for completion by 2010 and will a feature new stadium, an aquatic centre and water-sports facility.

The wholesale development of Marina Bay will also see that area turned into a water-sports centre, one protected from the vagaries of the tide by the Marina Barrage flood-control barrier.

THE ARTS

Set aside the achievements of somewhere comparable, such as Hong Kong, and Singapore's endeavours often seem rather bereft. Local painters and sculptors are largely anonymous, writers count publishing runs in the hundreds or low thousands, local movies rarely, if ever, reach large global audiences and theatre companies struggle with a lack of funds, short seasons and small audiences.

However, the city's artistic heart does beat, though faintly. The opening of the world-class Esplanade (p67) was a huge boost to the local arts scene (though small theatre groups might grumble that it swallowed up too much government money). The Singapore Symphony Orchestra and Singapore Chinese Orchestra perform regularly, while March sees the (hopefully) annual Mosaic Music Festival, featuring international acts perform everything from hip-hop to jazz to indie. There are also periodic outdoor concerts and music festivals at Fort Canning Park, which has hosted the likes of Jet, Incubus and even Black Sabbath.

Theatre and literature struggles. Though the Esplanade manages to attract luminaries such as the Royal Shakespeare Company for brief stints, local groups like Necessary Stage and Wild!Rice often stage productions with quality that veers wildly from the inspired to the mediocre. Furthermore, local audiences are far more likely to shell out money to see well-known international productions instead of supporting local groups.

In addition, theatre groups and artists, both local and foreign, still have to contend with censors, who block gratuitous sexual or religious content, and come down hard on any overt or implied criticism of the government. For example, two locally produced documentaries – on opposition figures JB Jeyaretnam and Chee Soon Juan – have been banned from local film festivals and their directors threatened with legal action.

If Singapore was once a caterpillar, flawlessly functional but uninspiring, it's now a butterfly, albeit one halfway out of its cocoon. Always a great place to eat, drink, dance and play, it's now shedding its conservatism in a big way and becoming one of Asia's cultural capitals.

There is no lack of places to drink and party (p163) in Singapore

ACCOMMODATION

Thanks to a recent boom in boutique and budget hotels, Singapore now has accommodation to suit all tastes and credit-card limits, from $20 dorm beds in Little India to the $1000-plus rooms at the Raffles Hotel, though average room rates have shot up in recent years. With a steady stream of visitors, there is no such thing as a low and high season in Singapore, but it's always advisable to book ahead, particularly if there's a big event in the city. If the inaugural Formula 1 Grand-Prix event held in September 2008 becomes annual, book months in advance, or reschedule your trip.

During big festivals such as Chinese New Year and Deepavali, booking hotels in Chinatown or Little India will put you at the centre of the festivities, while during National Day, in August, or Chingay, in February, hotels such as the towering cylindrical **Swissôtel, The Stamford** (www.singapore-stamford.swissotel.com), historical **Fullerton** (www.fullertonhotel.com) or sexy **Ritz-Carlton** (www.ritzcarlton.com/hotels/singapore) will give you bird's-eye views of the fireworks and the festivities.

For discount deals, check out (you guessed it) www.lonelyplanet.com, but also the plethora of online booking services including www.asiarooms.com or www.singaporehotels.com.

Singapore is a compact city with excellent public transport, so your choice of location is not crucial, but it's worth picking carefully. Shopaholics will prefer to be in the thick of the Orchard Rd action rather than lugging bags home every evening: the five-star functionality of the **Marriott** (www.singaporemarriott.com) or **Meritus Mandarin** (www.mandarin-singapore.com) puts you right on top of the malls, while the historic **Goodwood Park**

---

lonely planet | Hotels & Hostels

Need a place to stay? Find and book it at loneyplanet.com. More than 60 properties are featured for Singapore – each personally visited, thoroughly reviewed and happily recommended by a Lonely Planet author. From hostels to high-end hotels, we've hunted out the places that will bring you unique and special experiences. Read independent reviews by authors and other travellers, and get practical information including amenities, maps and photos. Then reserve your room simply and securely via Hotels & Hostels – our online booking service. It's all at lonelyplanet.com/hotels.

(www.goodwoodparkhotel.com) offers a little more ambience. Staying at the **YMCA** (www.ymcaih.com.sg), **SHA Villa** (www.sha.org.sg) or boutique backpacker retreat at **Hangout@Mt.Emily** (www.hangouthotels.com) will save you a little more money to pour into the shops.

Staying in more characterful Chinatown among the narrow lanes, restored shophouses and hawker centres will put you more in touch with the 'real' Singapore. Boutique hotels are the best options. The eccentric gothic **Scarlet Hotel** (www.thescarlethotel.com) might not suit everyone's taste, but the rooftop bar-restaurant views will melt your cynicism. Equally, almost painfully, hip are the **New Majestic Hotel** (www.newmajestichotel.com), whose rooms are individually designed by local artists, and **Hotel 1929** (www.hotel1929.com), where the rooms are the size of cupboards – very fashionable cupboards, though. More traditional shophouse restorations, where you won't feel quite so uncomfortable coming down to breakfast in tracksuit pants, are the **Berjaya Duxton** (www.berjayaresorts.com) and the baroque-themed **Royal Peacock** (www.royalpeacockhotel.com).

Little India specialises in forgettable two- and three-star accommodation, but the restored shophouse strip of the **Perak Hotel** (www.peraklodge.com) is a gem, while **The Inn Crowd** (www.the-inncrowd.com) has installed itself as a firm backpacker favourite.

Sentosa offers a mixed bunch. Pick of the pack are **The Sentosa** (www.thesentosa.com), a beautiful, elegant hotel with a priceless clifftop location and the **Amara Sanctuary** (www.amarasanctuary.com), housed in a former barracks. The ageing **Raja Sentosa** (www.shangri-la.com) is still the best spot for families and boasts magnificent views, but the Siloso Beach Resort, despite its alluring pool and waterfall, has attempted ecominimalist hip and ended up dank, drab and depressing.

BEST ON A BUDGET
> Betel Box (www.betelbox.com)
> Hangout@Mt Emily (www.hangouthotels.com)
> Sleepy Sam's (www.sleepysams.com)
> Summer Tavern (www.summertavern.com)
> The Inn Crowd (www.the-inncrowd.com)

BEST BOUTIQUE HOTELS
> Berjaya Duxton (www.berjayaresorts.com)
> Hotel 1929 (www.hotel1929.com)
> New Majestic Hotel (www.newmajestichotel.com)
> Royal Peacock Hotel (www.royalpeacockhotel.com)
> Scarlet Hotel (www.thescarlethotel.com)

FOOD

No subject arouses as much Singaporean passion, or is likelier to provoke an argument, than food. As KF Seetoh, writer and publisher of the *Makansutra* street-food bible, said: 'In Singapore, everyone is a food guide.' Seriously, it would be easier to win a consensus on climate change at the UN than it would be to find two Singaporeans who agree on the best place to eat something. All this bickering means one thing: there's an awful lot of good food out there. Singapore makes a convincing case for being the food capital of Asia. Whether or not that's true, eating is one of the greatest pleasures of this city and anyone who even dares set foot in an American junk-food chain here should be deported immediately and forbidden from returning.

For local food, there is no better place to go than the hawker centres (there are subtle distinctions between hawker centres, food centres, food courts, coffeeshops – but for brevity's sake we'll call any collection of stalls a hawker centre). These bustling agglomerations of Chinese, Indian, Malay and bastardised Western cuisines are the happiest consequence of Singapore's cultural stew. They are everywhere – in every shopping mall, on every street, in the public housing blocks, in the dingiest lane – and many are now embellished with Japanese, Korean, Thai and other regional cuisines.

In the perfect world, to visit one famous tourist-friendly hawker centre – be it the overenthusiastically developed Lau Pa Sat (p58), Maxwell Rd Hawker Centre (p59) or Newton Circus (p46) – would be enough to sample the best of everything. In reality, it's a fluid scene that's very hard to keep track of. Great stalls come and go, get in arguments with landlords or other stalls, find better premises. There's no guarantee that great *char kway teow* you had on your last visit will be there next time. So put your trust in the recommendation of your hotel receptionist or cab driver and plunge into somewhere new, or consult the highest authority and visit **Makansutra** (www .makansutra.com), whose guidebook is an essential companion for anyone serious about exploring hawker food in all its glory.

Be prepared though, sampling the best Singapore hawkers will at some point entail a visit to Geylang, the sleazy red-light district that doubles as the city's street-food capital, and where few Western tourists tread.

For those who prefer to go it alone, arriving at your first centre can be confusing (consult our guide, p59), but spotting the flavour of the month is simple. For many of us, the sight of a queue is an invitation to go elsewhere. For Singaporeans a long queue is like a homing beacon. They will happily stand for half an hour to get a popular dish, even if there's a perfectly delicious but less-busy alternative next door. That's what we call devotion.

While hawker food is Singapore's pride and joy, the city has a huge and fine collection of top restaurants. Excellent Italian and French restaurants abound, particular around the Chinatown area and in Holland Village. Japanese expats have colonised the excellent Cuppage Plaza eateries (and you know they can't be wrong), while homesick Thais head for the seedy surrounds, but superb food, at Golden Mile Complex (p87).

Self-caterers should head for supermarkets such as **Carrefour** (www.carrefour.com.sg) and **Marketplace** (www.coldstorage.com.sg), both of which have superb produce, while speciality shops such as Jones the Grocer (p121) keep the well-heeled supplied with infused oils and expensive cheeses.

BEST TOURIST-FREE HAWKER CENTRES
> Eng Seng Coffeeshop (p107)
> Hong Lim Complex (p58)
> Maxwell Rd Hawker Centre (p59)
> Old Airport Rd Food Centre (p110)
> Yong He Eating House (p111)

BEST STREETS FOR FOOD CRAWL
> Club St
> Geylang Rd
> Joo Chiat Rd/Joo Chiat Pl
> Race Course Rd
> Serangoon Rd

BEST FOR A CANDLELIT EUROPEAN DINNER
> Au Jardin Les Amis (p123)
> Il Lido (p100)
> L'Angelus (p58)
> Senso (p60)
> The Cliff (p101)

BEST FOR A FANCY CHINESE FEAST
> Lei Garden (p75)
> My Humble House (p75)
> Peach Garden (p60)
> Royal China (p75)
> Shang Palace (p46)

SNAPSHOTS

SHOPPING

Singapore's reputation as a cheap shopping destination, like its reputation for dullness, has more to do with its past than its present. For a long time, the likes of Bangkok, Kuala Lumpur and to some extent Hong Kong have eclipsed it for bargains, but Singapore still holds an edge in terms of convenience, while bargains can still be had on some clothing, watches, computer and electrical equipment and Asian antiques.

The Great Singapore Sale, held annually in June, is a good time for cut-price shopping, though the best deals are usually snapped up early. Though bargaining is possible in many places, visitors from other parts of Asia can find that freedom from the exhausting process of haggling comes as a blessed relief, especially on extended shopping excursions through the Grand Canyon of malls that line Orchard Rd (see boxed text, p42).

Get off Orchard Rd and there are many interesting finds to reward the adventurous. Little India (p86) is lined with gold, perfumes, cheap fabrics, spices and handicrafts. Book-ending Little India are the notorious edifices of bargain IT mall Sim Lim Sq (p89) and the 24-hour department store Mustafa Centre (p89), which is an experience in itself.

Down in the Arab Quarter are more fabrics, basket- and caneware shops, more jewellery, the hip boutiques of Haji Lane (see boxed text, p87) and the collection of art, handicraft and knick-knack shops on pedestrianised Bussorah St (see boxed text, p87). Nearby, the Bugis St Market is not a patch on the sleaze pit of old, but is a good hunting ground for cheap clothes and knock-offs.

Ignore the tourist stalls of Pagoda and Trengganu Sts in Chinatown. There are some real bargains to be found elsewhere in the area – particularly Asian art and artefacts, though many of the antiques are fake. For a department-store experience with a difference, amble through the five floors of Yue Hwa Chinese Products (p55).

A better place for art and antique hunting is the yuppie ghetto of Dempsey Rd (though the shops predate the area's yuppification), or the gloomy corridors of Tanglin Shopping Centre (not to be confused with Tanglin Mall, stomping ground of the Expatriate Wife).

BEST FOR THE UNEXPECTED FIND
> Bussorah St (boxed text, p87)
> Bugis St Market (p87)
> Haji Lane (boxed text, p87)
> Far East Plaza (boxed text, p42)
> Serangoon Rd and side streets (p86)

BEST FOR DESIGNER LABELS
> DFS Galleria (Map pp40–1, F3)
> Ngee Ann City (Map pp40–1, F4)
> Paragon (Map pp40–1, F4)
> Raffles City (Map pp68–9, F3)
> Tanglin Mall (Map pp40–1, D4)

BEST OFFBEAT MALLS
> Far East Plaza (Map pp40–1, F3)
> Holland Rd Shopping Centre (Map pp118–19, D4)
> Tanglin Shopping Centre (Map pp40–1, D3)
> The Heeren (Map pp40–1, G4)
> Vivocity (Map pp130–1, H6)

BEST STREET MARKETS
> Bugis St Market (p87)
> Sungei Rd Thieves Market (p90)

SINGAPORE FOR KIDS

If they can cope with the blazing heat and sapping humidity, kids of all temperaments seem to love Singapore. For the energetic and boisterous there's the Wild Wild Wet water park (p113), which is best visited on weekdays, though at weekends it can be combined with the ageing, but still fun, Escape Theme Park (p113) next door.

On Sentosa, after crossing the cable car they'll probably bankrupt you buying tickets to the Luge (p103), and if there's any money left, Underwater World (p100), Dolphin Lagoon (p100), the Flying Trapeze (p103) and Cineblast (p98) will soon swallow it up. In the city, the skyscraping attractions of the DHL Balloon (p94) and Singapore Flyer (p73) will tempt the brave, while over at East Coast Park thrillseekers will love the Ski 360° (p113) wakeboarding, kneeboarding and water-skiing park, followed by a spin on rented bikes or rollerblades.

The Singapore Zoo and Night Safari (see boxed text, p48) are very kid-friendly, as is the Bird Park (p138) over in Jurong, which is also home to the entertainingly educational Singapore Science Centre (p140). Next door are the Omni Theatre (p140), showing Imax films, and subzero Snow City (p142).

BEST FOR SHEER FUN
> Escape Theme Park (p113)
> Sentosa Luge (p103)
> Ski 360° (p113)
> Snow City (p142)
> Wild Wild Wet (p113)

BEST EDUCATIONAL DAYS OUT
> Jurong Bird Park (p138)
> Night Safari (p48)
> Singapore Science Centre (p140)
> Singapore Zoo (p48)

BARS & CLUBS

With countless bars, pubs and clubs of all descriptions, there's no excuse for a quiet night in. Singapore's rigid zoning policies mean bars and clubs are usually corralled into entertainment zones, which is good for pub crawls, but not so good if you're after a quiet neighbourhood drink.

Along Orchard Rd, the most popular haunt is Emerald Hill (see boxed text, p49), a collection of small, funky shophouse bars (which are all actually owned by the same company). In the Colonial District, an old convent compound has been beautifully, if a little cheekily, converted into the popular CHIJMES entertainment hub (Map pp68–9, E3).

The quays heave at night. Boat Quay (Map pp68–9, D5) draws the bankers and tourists (and the touts that hassle them), so nip one street back to the smaller bars and Hindi dance clubs on Circular Rd (Map pp68–9, D6). Redeveloped Clarke Quay (Map pp68–9, D5) has exploded in recent years, thanks partly to the Ministry of Sound phenomenon, though the whole area is a seething nest of dancing – check the Rupee Room (p78) and Cuba Libre (p76) – and drinking. Further upriver, Robertson Quay (Map pp68–9, A5) caters to the quieter, more sophisticated crowd.

The CBD falls quiet at night, but there's a pocket of activity in Far East Sq, which hosts the boozy Belgian bar Oosters (p62) and Kazbar (p62). For that neighbourhood drink, head to Club St (Map pp52–3, E4) in Chinatown, the BluJaz Café (p94) in the Arab Quarter, the Prince of Wales (p94) in Little India, or somewhere around Holland Rd or Bukit Timah.

The eight bars/clubs at St James Power Station (see boxed text, p134) complex in the southwest of the city, meanwhile, have emerged as a serious contender for Singapore's hottest nightspot.

BEST FOR DANCING
> Cuba Libre (p76)
> Ministry of Sound (p80)
> Movida (p134)
> Rupee Room (p78)
> Zouk (p81)

BEST FOR BEER
> Archipelago (p75)
> Brewerkz (p76)
> Oosters (p62)
> Paulaner Brauhaus (p77)
> Red Dot Brewhouse (p126)

FASHION

If asked to sum up Singapore's fashion sense in one phrase, 'smart casual' would be the most accurate. This is no Tokyo – the most adventurous dressers you're likely to see are the occasional, mostly Malay, teen goths, but even they are only conforming to a prescribed look. Singapore has, at least until a recent about-turn, always heavily discouraged individuality, which is strongly reflected in the local dress sense. Polo tees and jeans are all the rage, while teen girls and young women favour tiny denim shorts and miniskirts, often coupled with a singlet and ballet flats. Out in the heartlands, flip-flops (thongs), bermudas and T-shirts is the uniform of choice, while in the city, the sharp-dressed office dude will sport a striped shirt, black trousers, pointy or square-toed shoes and, of course, heavily gelled hair (not forgetting the phone clutched in one hand, or the mobile earpiece).

Despite this glaring absence of the unorthodox and the preoccupation with ubiquitous international designer brands, there are several notable hunting grounds for alternative wear. On Orchard Rd, head for the Heeren (Map pp40–1, G4) or Far East Plaza (Map pp40–1, F3), the former for local designers, the latter for cheap chic and the occasionally outlandish. Parco Bugis Junction maintains a small nest of local-designer outlets called Edge (p87), while across the road the new Bugis St Market sometimes yields a few surprises.

Top local names such as **Daniel Yam** (www.danielyam.com), **Anthea Chan** (www.perfectinblack.com) and, for the wildly offbeat, **K Mi Huang** (www.w-o-m-b.com) are a match for any international label.

Fashion show at the Paragon (see boxed text, p42) in Orchard Rd

LIVE MUSIC

The live-music scene in Singapore was once pretty dismal, but while there are still few original local bands of note, the situation has improved beyond measure.

Classical buffs are well-catered for, with regular performances by the Singapore Symphony Orchestra and Singapore Chinese Orchestra at the Esplanade (p67). Free outdoor concerts are held regularly on Fridays at the Esplanade and periodically on the Symphony Stage in the Botanic Gardens. Tickets for bigger concerts can be had from **Sistic** (www.sistic.com.sg) or **TicketCharge** (www.ticketcharge.com.sg).

Big pop and rock acts occasionally pass through, playing at the Singapore Indoor Stadium (Map p105, B3) or Fort Canning Park (Map p144, C3), but there are a host of great bands playing residences at places such as St James Power Station (p134), The Arena (p81) and Cuba Libre (p76), while venues such as Crazy Elephant (p79) and the Substation (Map pp68–9, E3) are the pick of the venues for local bands. The Prince of Wales (p94) in Little India regularly hosts decent local and expat outfits, as well as a patchy selection of earnest acoustic strummers (A pint of poetic misery sir? Coming right up). Check www.musicforgood.org for upcoming local concerts and events.

Options for jazz lovers are relatively limited, but Jazz@Southbridge (p80) is a must (we're big fans of their house rhythm section, though one of their pianists is painful). At weekends, BluJaz Café (p94) and Harry's Bar (p77) also put on credible performances and the Bellini Room at St James Power Station (p134) features irresistibly foot-tapping swing bands.

BEST FOR JAZZ
> Bellini Room (p134)
> BluJaz Café (p94)
> Harry's Bar (p77)
> Jazz@Southbridge (p80)

BEST FOR LIVE BANDS
> Crazy Elephant (p79)
> Movida (p134)
> Prince of Wales (p94)
> The Arena (p81)
> Wala Wala (p127)

ARCHITECTURE

Like many cities throughout the world, Singapore went through its own Dark Ages during the '60s and '70s, when the world fell in love with the functional concrete box. The result? The demolishing of much architectural heritage in a wrecking-ball frenzy.

Happily, sense eventually prevailed and there are preserved pockets of Singapore's wonderful architecture, though the concrete-box merchants still have plenty of work building the ubiquitous Housing & Development Board flats. The city's Colonial District is a treasure chest of tropical Palladian design, while Chinatown's remaining historical shophouses around Telok Ayer, Tanjong Pagar and the lanes off South Bridge Rd are heritage protected.

Around Joo Chiat, there are large pockets of traditional Peranakan shophouses – notable for their ornate facades and cool central courtyards.

Opinion is divided (as always) on the new buildings. Most people either love or hate the spiky durian-like Esplanade and the Norman Foster–designed 'spaceship' of the Supreme Court, while the oddly isolated, Gotham-style Parkview Sq puzzles a few. Worth spotting are the IM Pei–designed twin towers of the Gateway, designed to look two-dimensional from whatever angle you see it. For a masterpiece of melded modern and traditional design, visit the National Museum of Singapore (p70) – and check out those swinging chandeliers.

BEST MODERN BUILDINGS
> Esplanade (p67)
> National Museum of Singapore (p70)
> Parkview Sq (Map pp68–9, G2)
> Singapore Management University (Map pp68–9, F3)
> Supreme Court (Map pp68–9, E5)

BEST OLD BUILDINGS
> Asian Civilisations Museum (p67)
> Fullerton Hotel (Map pp68–9, F6)
> National Museum of Singapore (p70)
> Old Parliament House (The Arts House; Map pp68–9, E5)
> Raffles Hotel (p71)

GREEN SINGAPORE

A tiny island – with 4.5 million people stuffed into it – the mental image first-time visitors often have of Singapore is that of a human anthill, a concrete metropolis entirely given over to flats, industry and money making.

They soon discover otherwise. Quite apart from the huge number of city parks (p168), Singapore boasts wetlands, mangroves and, rather impressively, one of the only two patches of urban primary rainforest in the world, in the form of Bukit Timah Nature Reserve (p117).

The centre of the island is entirely devoted to forests and reservoirs, and the mangroves that once ringed the island are preserved in three main visitable pockets – Sungei Buloh Wetland Reserve (see boxed text, p141), Pasir Ris Park (p112) and Chek Jawa on Pulau Ubin (see boxed text, p114) – which teem with bird life, otters, monitor lizards and even a few crocodiles.

The forests of Bukit Timah and the Central Catchment Area (see Walking Tour, p146) are the best places to spot long-tailed macaques, flying lemurs, pythons, lizards and hundreds of bird species.

Singapore is slowly converting to the environmental cause, though a noticeable recent worsening in traffic volume and the slow adoption of recycling must surely threaten its green policies and its generally good air quality. The government produces three-yearly revisions to its 2012 Green Plan, which commits the island to reducing carbon-dioxide emissions, water consumption and air pollution, and improving waste management.

The island cannot control the actions of its neighbours, though, and from June to September the thick, pungent haze drifting from Indonesian plantation fires can send air quality plummeting for weeks on end.

Couple having a picnic at the Singapore Botanic Gardens (p117)

PARKS

It's the first thing many visitors notice: the extravagant botanical displays lining the expressway leading from Changi Airport. It isn't just window dressing either. Singapore has some serious greenery.

One of the happier consequences of strict government control has been the creation of hundreds of city and neighbourhood parks. They aren't just vacant patches of land grudgingly cordoned off from eager developers by an apathetic local council either.

Singapore's parks are often masterpieces of design and landscaping, from the tiniest urban oasis such as Telok Ayer Garden (Map pp52–3, F4) to the forests of Kent Ridge Park (p129) and Labrador Nature Reserve (p129) and the large manicured spaces of East Coast Park (see boxed text, p112). Expect to find bicycle paths, unvandalised benches, exercise routes complete with equipment, lily ponds, foot-reflexology paths, bird-watching hides, mangrove walks, restaurants, museums, spice gardens and vegetable patches, dog runs and barbecue pits. At the time of writing, a huge network of park connectors is under construction (www .nparks.gov.sg/park_connectors.asp) that will enable cyclists and runners to move around the island without encountering a road.

To enter one of these wonderful places is to believe that, for all the cynicism the Singaporean social experiment arouses, this is a city that has passionately pursued the restorative power of green space in a crowded environment and, just perhaps, has its citizens' welfare at heart.

BEST WATERFRONT PARKS
> East Coast Park (see boxed text, p112)
> Labrador Nature Reserve (p129)
> MacRitchie Reservoir Nature Park (see Walking Tour, p146)
> Pasir Ris Park (p112)

BEST IN THE CITY TO ESCAPE THE CITY
> Fort Canning Park (p39)
> Kent Ridge Park (p129)
> Labrador Nature Reserve (p129)
> Mt Faber Park (p129)
> Telok Ayer Garden (Map pp52–3, F4)

CELLULOID

Singaporeans are avid movie-goers and proudly boast that more movie tickets are sold here per capita than anywhere else in the world. Visitors need to arm themselves with warm clothing and a large reserve of patience, however: Singaporeans love to chat and rustle their snack packets during movies, and the air-con is often so high it'll make your teeth chatter.

Hollywood rules here – the more mainstream the better and in the city centre, huge crowds queue up for tickets to the latest blockbuster, romantic comedy, or CGI-animals crowd-pleaser. To avoid frustration, booking in advance at **Golden Village** (www.gv.com.sg) lets you skip the queue.

The city's growing sophistication has seen a couple of options emerge for international and alternative movies: Cinema Europa at Golden Village Vivocity (p132) and the hip, luxurious Screening Room (p65) in Chinatown. Once a year, in April, the Singapore International Film Festival (p25) showcases more than a hundred independent movies from all over the world.

Golden Village's Gold Class at Vivocity has waiter service and plush reclining seats, but the higher ticket prices mean the movie had better be worth it.

Singaporean cinema has never quite found a voice or style of its own. Local productions are derivative and vary widely in quality, which, given the island's negligible output, it can scarcely afford (see p185).

BEST CINEMAS TO AVOID
> Cathay Cineleisure Orchard – takes forever to get upstairs
> Eng Wah Toa Payoh – crowd noise
> Lido at Shaw House – long weekend queues, very cold

BEST OFFBEAT AND LUXURY CINEMAS
> Cinema Europa at Vivocity (p132)
> Golden Village's Gold Class at Vivocity (p132)
> The Picturehouse at Cathay (Map pp68–9, D2)
> The Screening Room (p65)

SNAPSHOTS

MUSEUMS

Singapore is almost embarrassingly well-endowed with museums, from the tiny and obscure to the grand and meaty, many of them clustered around the Colonial District.

There's a certain understandable preoccupation with Singapore history, to the point of repetition, and the political overtones sometimes get a little heavy, but by and large they are excellent.

The city's pride and joy is the Asian Civilisations Museum (p67) – they took George W Bush there, and doubtless he revelled in the academic pursuit of foreign cultural understanding. Second in the pecking order is the National Museum of Singapore (p70), magnificently restored and kitted out with an impressive modern annex. The Singapore Art Museum (p71) nearby focuses on the regional art experience, but also houses the works of names such as Rothko.

The anguish of Singapore's WWII experience is marked in several places (see p19). This watershed period in the country's history is covered in depth over several museums and commemorated at several sites: including Fort Siloso on Sentosa, Memories at Bukit Chandu at Kent Ridge Park, Memories at Old Ford Factory in Bukit Timah, as well as at the National Museum and Images of Singapore on Sentosa. The trauma of occupation, and Singapore's tetchy postwar relations with its larger neighbours, have inspired its obsession with security today.

Of the specific cultural museums, the Chinatown Heritage Centre (p51) is the best, followed by its sister Peranakan Museum (p70), which studies the region's mixed Malay-Chinese ethnic community.

MUST NOT MISS
> Asian Civilisations Museum (p67)
> Fort Siloso (p98)
> National Museum of Singapore (p70)
> Singapore Art Museum (p71)

BEST FOR THE WAR EXPERIENCE
> Changi Memorial & Chapel (p106)
> Fort Siloso (p98)
> Reflections At Bukit Chandu (p132)
> The Battle Box (p39)
> Kranji War Memorial (p177)

GAY & LESBIAN SINGAPORE

Thumping gay clubs, saunas and massage parlours in discreet doorways, lesbians holding hands in the street, drag queens on the TV – hold on, is this really uptight, repressive Singapore?

As with many things in this city, its stance on homosexuality is enigmatic. Male homosexuality is illegal, yet its many gay clubs, bars and saunas – centred on Chinatown – operate openly and largely unmolested by police. Even Lee Kuan Yew, architect of Singapore's official moral code, recently made some veiled conciliatory noises suggesting the government's antigay stance may be outdated.

Having said that, the government is not going to open the floodgates just yet. Police refused further permits for two highly successful annual gay parties that had attracted regional attention: Nation and SnowBall. The prime minister backed them up, saying Singapore was not ready for the promotion of gay lifestyles.

For the best and latest information and listings, check www.utopia-asia .com, or try local lifestyle site www.trevvy.com (which replaced the banned www.sgboy.com) or regional gay and lesbian site www.fridae.com.

As for lesbians, legally they don't exist, which means the law must be walking around with eyeshades on, because you'd be hard pressed to spend more than a few hours in any street or mall without seeing lesbian couples, often walking hand in hand, sometimes more, and attracting no obvious attention. In fact, there is unlikely to be a city in Asia, perhaps even the world, where lesbians are more visible.

In 2007, the government banned an Xbox game that features a human-alien, all-female kissing scene. Evidently embarrassed by the worldwide headlines the ban generated, the government relented.

SNAPSHOTS

SPORTS

Despite the roaringly hot and humid year-round conditions in their city, Singaporeans are keen on outdoor pursuits.

Cyclists can arrange rides with the **ANZA club** (www.anzacycling.com) or through the **Cycleworx shop** (www.cycleworx.com). The **Singapore Amateur Cycling Association** (www.cycling.org.sg) has lots of information. Mountain bikers can use the trail at Bukit Timah Nature Reserve (p117), but there are no bikes for hire there.

Runners can hook up with the approachable **MacRitchie Runners** (www .mr25.org.sg), who meet up for runs nearly every day. Endurance sports are very popular and there are regular races, usually at East Coast Park. Check the **Triathlon Association site** (www.triathlonsingapore.org) for information.

Even with space contraints, Singapore has somehow found room for a surprising number of golf courses, but green fees for nonmembers are high, ranging from $90 on less-prestigious courses such as Jurong Country Club to $450 for a weekend round at the championship Serapong course (p103).

Rock climbers will find the Dairy Farm Quarry a challenge, or try the indoor 'rock gym' at **Climb Adventure** (www.climbadventure.com).

Given the oily sea that surrounds the island, Singapore is not great for beach swimming, but if your hotel doesn't have a pool, the city's public pools, such as the River Valley Swimming Complex (Map pp68–9, C4), are clean and cheap. Card-carrying sailors and windsurfers have the choice of several sea sports clubs – see www.water-venture.org.sg for more information.

For wakeboarders, water skiers and kneeboarders, the Ski 360° (p113) cable-ski lagoon at East Coast Park is a must.

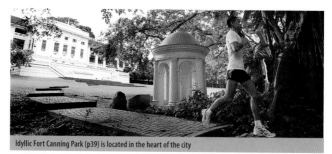

Idyllic Fort Canning Park (p39) is located in the heart of the city

ACM EMPRESS PLACE - OPEN NOW

The iconic Asian Civilisations Museum (p67) stands picturesque against the Singapore River

BACKGROUND
HISTORY

Malay legend tells of a Sumatran prince Sang Nila Utama sheltering from a storm on the island of Temasek and spotting a lion – a good omen that prompted the prince to found a city there called Singapura (Lion City). It is of course highly unlikely that lions ever roamed the island's forests, but it's somehow an appropriate tale for a city so adept at creating mythologies.

Actual records of Singapore's early history are sketchy. Originally it was an insignificant port squeezed between muscular neighbours Sumatra and Melaka, and there are records of Chinese traders visiting the island, which appeared on Chinese maps as Pu-Luo-Chong as far back as AD 300.

Singapore's official history begins in 1819 with the arrival of Sir Stamford Raffles, who was declared Singapore's founder in the 1970s in order to 'neutrally' settle rival claims by local Malays and Chinese. With no claims to indigenous rights, Singapore has been free to do as it pleases with its land.

COLONIAL CONQUEST

In the late 18th century Britain began looking for a harbour in the Strait of Melaka that would usurp its Portuguese and Dutch competitors and secure its trade routes between China, India and the Malay world.

Young Stamford Raffles arrived in Singapore in 1819 to find the Johor empire divided, with two contenders for the sultanship. The Dutch favoured one candidate, so Raffles backed the rival contender Hussein and proclaimed him sultan, clinching the deal by signing a treaty with an eminent *temenggong* (senior judge). This exchange ended with the 1824 cash buyout of Hussein and the judge, transferring Singapore's ownership to the British East India Company. The last sultan, Ali Iskander Shah, was given an *istana* (palace) in Kampong Glam that still stands there today, though the family moved out in 1999 and the building now houses the Malay Heritage Centre.

Raffles laid down the initial plans for the development of the free-trade port, which had attracted thousands of immigrant traders and merchants. Spotting the potential for conflict, Raffles delineated ethnic districts in his city plans that remain today. The streets of Chinatown,

Little India, the Arab Quarter and the Colonial District are just as Raffles drew them nearly 200 years ago.

The man charged with turning these plans into physical reality was town surveyor George Drumgoole Coleman, a talented Irishman who was responsible for the city's central road network and many of its finest buildings. He skilfully adapted the Palladian style to fit the tropical climate, designing buildings such as Caldwell House in CHIJMES (now a pleasant spot for an evening beer), Old Parliament House, Armenian Church and St Andrew's Cathedral, as well as Thian Hock Keng Temple and the Hajjah Fatimah Mosque.

THE EARLY COLONY

Singapore was soon teeming with Chinese immigrants. Back in 1879, European traveller Isabella Bird noted the 'resistless, overpowering, astonishing Chinese element, which is gradually turning Singapore into a Chinese city!'

Many of these Chinese, mostly from China's southern provinces, landed at the Thian Hock Keng Temple in Chinatown (which was on the seashore at that time), then were quickly absorbed into their respective communities by the clan societies, whose headquarters once lined Club St, where a few remain.

The indolence and heat-induced torpor Bird described in other parts of Asia and the Pacific were entirely absent from early Singapore. From the beginning, it was dynamic and driven, its population inspired into frenzied activity by the lure of fortune. The British forged good trading relations with the Straits-born Chinese-Malays, known as Peranakans, who found an identity in the Union Jack, British law and citizenship.

Conditions, except for the British ensconced in their breezy colonial villas, were tough. A visit to the Chinatown Heritage Centre (p51) provides an accurate insight into life in that neighbourhood, riddled as it was with bad sanitation, disease, British Empire–sponsored opium addiction, gang warfare and prostitution. Violence was common and policing minimal.

THE BELLY OF THE CARP
During the early boom years of Singapore, Chinese traders favoured Boat Quay because at that point the river was shaped like the belly of the carp, which is an auspicious symbol for business in Chinese belief. In this case, they were often right.

In 1887, the interracial tensions Raffles had meant to forestall with his segregated town plan led to riots, not for the last time.

But the city was booming. Along the Singapore River, the sloping tiled roofs where you can now sit for a few drinks and a nice meal once sheltered the *towkays* (businessmen), who set up trading houses along the bank for goods such as rubber, tin, rice, coffee and steel, turning the area into the economic engine room of the city. The bumboats that ferry tourists up and down the river were in the mid- to late-1800s so tightly jammed around Boat Quay you could almost have crossed the river by stepping between them.

By the 1930s and early 1940s, the rumblings of international politics began to filter into the city. The Indian independence movement and communist struggles in China captured Singapore's imagination, causing the British a few palpitations. However, whatever winds of change were rustling Singapore society were soon blown away by the storm of WWII.

WWII & THE JAPANESE INVASION

Some historians label the Japanese occupation of Singapore as the key moment in the decline of the British Empire, the moment that tore apart the myth of British military might on an island once viewed as an impregnable fortress.

The impact of the occupation on the collective memory of this island cannot be underestimated. Just look at the sheer number of museums and memorials (p170) devoted to the memory and study of the invasion.

General Yamashita Tomoyuki pushed his thinly stretched army into the northwest of Singapore on 15 February 1942. Around 140,000 Australian, New Zealand, British and oft-overlooked Indian, Dutch and Malay troops were killed or imprisoned in the invasion.

If the invasion was a humiliation for the British Empire, it was a disaster for many of those who lived through it. The Allied soldiers were herded into the horrors of the Changi POW camp or shipped off to the worse fate of building the Death Railway in Thailand.

Singaporean Chinese paid an equally heavy price. Thousands of Chinese (Singapore claims 50,000; Japan says 6000) were targeted for torture and mass execution at Sentosa and Changi Beach, where a memorial marks the spot of the slaughter.

Japanese rule was harsh in Singapore, temporarily renamed Syonan (Light of the South). Malays and Indians were subject to systematic

THE KRANJI WAR MEMORIAL

The Allied **war cemetery** (☎ 6269 6158; 9 Woodlands Rd; admission free; ⏰ 7am-6pm; Ⓜ Kranji MRT, 🚌 170) contains around 4000 graves and memorial walls bearing the inscribed names of 24,346 people whose bodies were never recovered. There are registers listing the dead by the memorial walls and visitors books at the entrance. Like all war cemeteries, it's a distressing sight. The one heart-warming aspect of the place is the team of diligent groundsmen that keeps the place in an immaculate state.

abuse. Inflation skyrocketed; food, medicines and other essentials became scarce, and starvation ensued.

When the war ended with the atomic bombing and Japan's surrender on 14 August 1945, Singapore was passed back into British control. Despite an official apology in 1991 and generous monetary loans, Singapore has never forgotten the Japanese, a fact you only have to visit somewhere like Reflections at Bukit Chandu (p132) to witness.

POSTWAR ALIENATION

The British were welcomed back to Singapore but their right (and ability) to rule was now in seriously in question. Postwar poverty, unemployment and nationalist sentiment provided a groundswell of support for communism, and Singapore moved slowly towards self-government.

By the early 1950s the 'communist threat' had waned but left-wing activity was still on the upswing. One of the rising stars of this era was Lee Kuan Yew, a third-generation Straits-born Chinese who had studied law at Cambridge. The socialist People's Action Party (PAP) was founded in 1954 with Lee as secretary-general.

Under arrangements for internal self-government, PAP won a majority of seats in the new Legislative Assembly in 1959, and Lee Kuan Yew became the first Singapore prime minister – a title he held for the next 31 years.

INDEPENDENT SINGAPORE

By the early 1960s Britain had devised a way to withdraw regional colonial rule by creating the new state of Malaysia, uniting Malaya with Sabah, Sarawak and Singapore. In 1965 Singapore was expelled, largely due to Malay fears of Chinese dominance. Singapore reluctantly

SIR STAMFORD RAFFLES

Even viewed from today's anticolonial perspective, Sir Stamford Raffles was an extraordinary individual. Only 45 when he died of a probable brain tumour, the man who started as a humble clerk was an accomplished naturalist, cultural scholar, enlightened colonial governor, Malay speaker, founder of the London Zoo and the visionary who effectively created the city of Singapore. But he ended his life in frustration and unhappiness, having lost four of his five children and having the East India Company refuse his pension. The vicar who buried Raffles had interests in slave plantations and refused him a memorial stone, because he objected to Raffles' friendship with abolitionist William Wilberforce. Six years after his death, his accomplishments were recognised with a statue in Westminster Abbey.

struck out on its own and vigorously survived. Despite having no natural resources, under Lee Kuan Yew it quickly entrenched itself as a manufacturing, trading and financial centre, transforming itself into an economic powerhouse.

In the process, Lee embarked on an experiment in social engineering that has been famous and infamous in equal measure, attracting admiration from some quarters (foreign governments eager to replicate its level of control reportedly send frequent delegations to study the 'Singapore system') and hostility from others.

There have been less imposed strict laws on Singapore's population (the chewing gum ban and jaywalking laws being the most well-known, but by no means the most severe) and political opposition has been ruthlessly quashed.

Lee stepped down in 1990, handing over to Goh Chok Tong, an erudite, avuncular but equally tough figure sometimes unfairly dismissed as a place-holder for Lee Kuan Yew's oldest son, Lee Hsien Loong, who became PM in 2004.

Lee the Younger faces challenges perhaps as tough as those that greeted his father in 1965. Maintaining Singapore's strength involves remodelling itself as a global city and a hub for anything and everything: transport, high finance, IT, higher education, medical travel, digital media, the arts, conferences, tourism, biomedical engineering. For this, it needs to import thousands more professionals and labourers, but in the process maintain the traditional social order and values that bind the island's society. Singapore is a city in flux. It's fascinating to watch it in process – and it will be fascinating to see where it goes.

LIFE AS A SINGAPOREAN

Being part of the Singapore miracle has bestowed upon many of the island's residents a level of economic prosperity and freedom their grandparents, and even parents, could never have imagined. They enjoy decent education, health care, infrastructure, low levels of crime, clean water, plentiful food and freedom to travel – a modern lifestyle millions of citizens in countries neighbouring Singapore aspire to, but will struggle to achieve in this generation.

The average Singaporean will live in a privately owned, government-built unit known as an Housing & Development Board (HDB) flat, which will have been purchased using money from their compulsory government savings account, known as the CPF. Life usually involves early starts and long hours of work that helps pay off hefty home and possibly car loans – Singapore has the costliest cars in the world – though the domestic load is often lightened by many with the employment of a live-in maid from Indonesia or the Philippines.

Children are pushed hard from a young age and spend long hours at school, and are often thrust into extracurricular activities in the manic rush for places at top schools and universities.

Each of the HDB 'towns' cram in many thousands of families, and a sense of community that once thrived in the old kampong (villages), which were torn down to make way for them, has been harder to replicate. As a Singaporean you are bombarded with efforts to forge a strong national and racial identity, and persistently badgered by official campaigns – Speak Good English! Speak Mandarin! Be More Considerate! Be Spontaneous! Be More Careful! Drive Courteously! A well-oiled media spin machine churns out whatever stories are deemed necessary to reinforce the political and social agenda.

Local councils try to forge community bonds through the organisation of regular events at the 'void decks' (empty areas beneath blocks of flats) or community centres, where you'll often see large congregations of people tucking into meals and being entertained by singers on temporary stages.

To enjoy this level of comfort, Singaporeans have been required to enter into a social contract: namely, the government delivers prosperity and security to them and, in return, they don't rock the boat. The explicit message spun to every Singaporean, particularly through the country's docile media, is that the country's prosperity depends entirely on the maintenance of the political status quo.

Privately many people – especially those battling rising poverty, a growing income gap and a rapidly increasing cost of living – complain bitterly about the situation, but few dare do much else, because the stories of what has happened to those who have openly challenged the political or social order are ingrained in the national consciousness: lawsuits, bankruptcy, jail, ruin. And in reality, deep down even those who grumble often support the system, because the alternatives are presented as all too frightening.

Though many long-term residents speak of a subtle climate of fear, most short-term visitors will find Singaporeans on the whole to be friendly, helpful and engaging, often diffident but often ready for a good laugh.

It is true, though, that years of well-meaning multicultural social engineering seems to have engendered an acute preoccupation with questions of race and identity, and don't be surprised if some aspect of your behaviour is interpreted not as a personal characteristic, but as the indelible product of your racial identity. The fatal race riots that fractured the city in the '60s may be far in the past, but they are kept fresh in the political memory, and the message of multiculturalism and religious plurality is continually reinforced through the local councils, annual festivals and the media.

Beneath the surface, remnants of racial enmity simmer, but economic success and harsh punishments for those who voice racist views has kept a lid on them. Even so, levels of hostility towards foreigners, whether it's the *ang moh* (Westerners) or *bangla* (labourers from the Indian subcontinent), exist, though it's more often openly expressed as ridicule rather than outright dislike.

Food and football are by far the best ways to dip a toe into Singaporean culture. Food is a local passion, an indispensable part of a happy life, and Singaporeans devote hours to eating, thinking about eating, or talking about where to eat. In a city preoccupied with status and hierarchy, food is the great social leveller – the love of eating will see managing directors pull up plastic chairs next to tables of foreign construction workers (though proximity does not translate as interaction). Choose a local dish, ask someone where is the best place to find it and, presto, you have a conversation.

Anyone with an interest in football – or more specifically English Premier League football – will also find instant common ground with most Singaporean males, and many females, who have adopted club partisanship with a level of passionate devotion that rivals the English (or Thais, or Malaysians, or Chinese!). Coffeeshops and pubs are packed out for games, though of course physical violence between rival fans is almost unheard of.

Beneath all the modernity and apparent Westernisation, strict Confucian family ideals still hold sway. Though there are signs these ideals are in decline, filial piety for Chinese Singaporeans is still an overarching philosophy, which sees many people living in extended families, or at least living close to their parents. It is explicitly expected that citizens extend the same level of self-sacrifice to the nation.

One obvious manifestation of this principle is national service. All Singaporean men live under the constant shadow (or beam of sunshine, depending on who you talk to) of military service. As well as their compulsory two years of duty, all males are required to be on standby and most have to do a stint for a couple of weeks a year.

GOVERNMENT & POLITICS

Politics in Singapore is everywhere and nowhere. Everywhere, in the sense that, with the increasingly significant exception of the web pages that pop up on Singapore's computer screens, everything you see, read and hear has at some point felt the guiding hand of government upon it. Nowhere, in the sense that what much of the world understands by politics – the ebb and flow of conflicting opinions and ideas in a public forum – is almost nonexistent.

The People's Action Party has held power in Singapore since 1959 and has been virtually the sole political force since 1965, when the island was kicked out of the Malay Federation after an uneasy alliance forged in 1963. Then Prime Minister Lee Kuan Yew famously cried on television the day Singapore was left to fend for itself, but he's shed few tears since.

The white-clad party he led with steely paternalism maintains total control to this day. Opposition voices such as JB Jeyaratnam, Francis Seow and Chee Soon Juan have been dragged through the courts and financially ruined by lawsuits – a means of removing them from the political process, since bankrupts aren't allowed to run for election. The argument, which many Singaporeans understandably find persuasive, is that a successful government doesn't need challenging. (It might also

UNCLE HARRY

While the nascent Singapore city was created by the vision of Sir Stamford Raffles, modern Singapore is undoubtedly the vision of Lee Kuan Yew. A Straits-born Chinese known as Harry Lee, he was educated at the prestigious Raffles Institution and then in law at Cambridge University. He was, he said, raised to be 'the equal of any Englishman'. Despite resigning as PM in 1990, he still oversees and directs policy in his role as Minister Mentor, and once said: 'Even if you are going to lower me into the grave and I feel that something is wrong, I'll get up.'

be argued that a successful government should be a little less insecure about open criticism.)

Elections are a carefully managed affair. Rallies, speeches, posters and manifestos present all the trappings of the democratic process, but in reality opposition parties have little chance of winning power.

Even so, the PAP only won 66% of the vote at the last election in 2006, a fall of nearly 9% from the previous election, though they still took 82 of parliament's 84 seats.

For the first time since 1988, the PAP was not automatically returned to power on nomination day via uncontested seats. The constituencies of Hougang and Potong Pasir, despite heavy inducements from the PAP in the form of promised HDB upgrading projects, remained defiantly in opposition hands.

The opposition Worker's Party attracted huge crowds to its rallies before the poll, filling two sports stadiums, but the stories of these rallies never appeared in the local press.

Which brings us to the internet. The PAP is slowly waking up to the realities of the online world, but its reactions to events often betrays a mind-set stuck in the days when most information channels could be managed. Photos of those 2006 Worker's Party rallies were up on the internet within hours, just one example of how the web has given birth to a new era of political discussion and a forum for dissent in Singapore.

Visit http://singabloodypore.rsfblog.org and see the sheer number of links to other political blogs. Some of them are wild rants, others are considered, thoughtful analyses.

Whether or not this is indicative of any fundamental grass-roots change remains to be seen. As long as Singapore remains prosperous, the PAP is likely to remain politically secure, but as that prosperity is leaving an ever-growing local underclass behind, even that may not be taken for granted.

ENVIRONMENT

Sir Stamford Raffles would hardly recognise it. There are few reminders now of the Singapore of old – thickly forested, ringed with swampy mangrove, patrolled by snakes and tigers and highly malarial. The only spots where it's still possible to see Singapore's indigenous environment are Pulau Ubin (see boxed text, p114), Bukit Timah (p117) and the Sungei Buloh Wetland Reserve (p141). The rest of the island has been stripped, cleaned, moulded, flattened and enlarged to squeeze in people, roads and industries.

The effect of all this on the island's ecology has naturally been dramatic. The last tiger was shot in the 1930s (some place this event in Choa Chu Kang in the west of the island, others at the Raffles Hotel). Other wildlife remains in the forests that dominate the centre of the island: macaques, monitor lizards, flying lemurs, pythons, the occasional cobra and anteater, 364 bird species and around 935 kinds of insect, though new ones continue to be discovered.

Under the sea, land reclamation, the constant flow of container vessels and massive heavy industry has combined to destroy much of the country's marine ecosystem. Though pockets of reef remain offshore from islands such as St John's, the 'forests of coral' described by Isabella Bird in 1879 are long gone.

Singapore's flora is more prodigious. One naturalist estimated that there were more plant varieties in Singapore than in the whole of North America, despite the fact that only a tiny percentage of the original forest and mangrove cover remains.

HANDS OFF OUR SAND

In January 2007, the Indonesian government sprung a surprise when it announced it was banning exports of sand to Singapore. This sand, used for Singapore's massive land-reclamation projects and construction industry, was suddenly in short supply, sparking huge price increases and palpitations in high office. Officially, Indonesia said the ban had been enacted to protect the country's environment, but people familiar with Indonesia's somewhat patchy environmental record said it was more likely a tool to pressure Singapore to sign an extradition treaty that Indonesia hoped would help it recover billions of dollars in embezzled Indonesian funds allegedly secreted into Singapore's financial system. Negotiations did begin over an extradition treaty, but the ban remains in place. Besides, sand extraction had already decimated large parts of the Riau archipelago's marine ecosystem, begging the question: why now?

FURTHER READING

The wealth of historical and political literature on Singapore is a testament not only to the importance of its strategic role, but the fascination this tiny and formerly seedy port city inspired, particularly among the Europeans, who account for the vast majority of historical and fictional writing. Local fiction has always been a little thin on the ground, but there has been a recent resurgence in local writing. Many of the following will be available in Kinokuniya (p39), Borders or the academic **Select Books** (p42; www.selectbooks.com.sg), and though some are out of print (or banned) they are available secondhand through Amazon.

Travellers' Singapore, a collection of accounts taking in a broad sweep from the early 1800s to 1942, and the similar *Travellers' Tales of Old Singapore* are the most entertaining way to get an overview of the island's past.

Raffles, by Maurice Collis, is by far the best biography of the great scholar and statesman, while the most damning account of the fall of the island to the Japanese in 1942 is *Singapore: The Pregnable Fortress* by Peter Elphick.

It isn't quite the *Little Red Book* – it's hardly little, for one thing – but a copy of Lee Kuan Yew's *Singapore Story* is obligatory for anyone wanting to understand not only how the Singapore miracle came about, but also the thinking of the man who masterminded it.

For a glimpse into the darker side of that same miracle, *Lee's Law*, by Chris Lydgate, offers a disturbing account of the rise and systematic destruction of Singapore's most famous dissenter, lawyer and opposition member JB Jeyaretnam. James Minchin's *No Man Is An Island* presents a broad critical study of Lee Kuan Yew. Another lawyer, former Law Society president, Francis Seow, has penned two similar books: *To Catch A Tartar*, about his own nightmarish experiences on the wrong side of Mr Lee's favour, and *Beyond Suspicion? The Singapore Judiciary*. Not surprisingly, none of these books is available in Singapore.

Singapore has been graced by some of Western literature's finest writers. James Clavell's *King Rat*, set in the notorious Japanese POW camp at Changi, JG Farrell's *The Singapore Grip*, set in the same era, and Paul Theroux's rowdy *Saint Jack* are among the most widely read.

The city's cultural commentators have long bemoaned and debated its sparse collection of local literary luminaries, but writers such as the late 'Voice of Singapore' Goh Sin Tub *(Ghosts of Singapore* and *The Ghost Lover of Emerald Hill)*, Philip Jeyaretnam *(Tigers in Paradise, Raffles Place Ragtime)*, Catherine Lim *(The Bondmaid)* and Tan Hwee Hwee *(Mammon Inc)* are well worth reading for insights into how Singapore views itself.

FILMS

Singaporean cinematic achievement in the past has been patchy, to say the least. Lack of money, lack of interest, dearth of creative talent, lack of official encouragement and many other explanations have been cited. Another explanation could be that societies need an underbelly on which cinematic art can feed and, unlike somewhere comparable in size such as Hong Kong, Singapore either lacked that colourful underbelly, or was simply unhappy about the idea of portraying social problems, particularly in a medium with so much power to shape perceptions.

Recently, in line with government efforts to foster a more creative society, money has been poured into local movies, through the conduit of the Singapore Film Commission and local deep-pocket production houses such as Raintree Productions, with mixed success.

The best local director is probably Eric Khoo, whose *Mee Pok Man, 12 Storeys,* and *Be With Me* are set in the island's 'heartlands' and have been well received. The latter two were hits at the Cannes Film Festival.

Jack Neo boasts Singapore's three highest-grossing local productions. *Money No Enough* focused on the dark side of the heartlands in the shape of the loan sharks who patrol these vast estates and feed on the impoverished. *I Not Stupid* is an amusing and biting look at Singapore society through its pushy hothouse education system, while the sequel *I Not Stupid Too* was more successful commercially, though not as satirical.

Young director Royston Tan came to prominence in 2005, when his film *15: The Movie*, which dealt with drug abuse and wayward youth, was cut by the censors. As always, the act of censorship won the film more attention and acclaim, making Tan something of a local celebrity, especially after he lampooned the censors in the musical sequence *Cut*. Tan's subsequent efforts, such as the musical comedy *881*, have veered towards the mainstream.

DIRECTORY
TRANSPORT
ARRIVAL & DEPARTURE
AIR

Unless you're coming from Tioman Island (in which case you land at Seletar Airport), all flights arrive at one of the four terminals at **Changi Airport** (☎ 6542 1122, flight information 1800 542 4422; www.changiairport.com) about 20km east of the city centre. There are three main terminals and a Budget Terminal.

Bus

Public bus 36 runs from Terminals 1, 2 and 3 to Orchard Rd and the Colonial District ($1.70, one hour). They leave roughly every 15 minutes, the first departing at 6.09am and the last just after midnight.

Faster and more convenient are the airport shuttle buses (adult/child $9/6, 20 to 40 minutes) that leave from all main terminal arrival halls and drop passengers at any hotel, except for those on Sentosa and at Changi Village. They leave from Terminals 1 and 2 and the Budget Terminal (midnight to 6.15pm, every 30 minutes, 6.15pm to midnight, every 15 minutes) and Terminal 3 (6am to 10am and 6pm to 2am, every 15 minutes, 11am-6pm, 2am to 6am, every 30 minutes). Booking desks are in the arrival halls.

Train

The clean and efficient Mass Rapid Transit (MRT) is the best budget way to get into town. The station is located below Terminals 2 and 3, the fare to Raffles Pl is $2.70/$1.50 per adult/child (including a $1 refundable deposit) and the journey takes around 35 minutes. You have to change trains at Tanah Merah (just cross the platform). The first train leaves at 5.30am and the last goes at 12.06am.

CLIMATE CHANGE & TRAVEL

Travel – especially air travel – is a significant contributor to global climate change. At Lonely Planet, we believe that all who travel have a responsibility to limit their personal impact. As a result, we have teamed with Rough Guides and other concerned industry partners to support Climate Care, which allows people to offset the greenhouse gases they are responsible for with contributions to energy-saving projects and other climate-friendly initiatives in the developing world. Lonely Planet offsets all staff and author travel.

For more information, turn to the responsible travel pages on www.lonelyplanet.com. For details on offsetting your carbon emissions and a carbon calculator, go to www.climatecare.org.

Taxi

Taxi lines at Changi are usually fast-moving and efficient, even at the Budget Terminal, and you rarely have to wait long. The fare structure is brain-meltingly complicated, but count on spending anywhere between $18 and $35 into the city centre, depending on the time of travel. The most expensive times are between 5pm and 6am, when a whole smorgasbord of surcharges kick in.

A limousine transfer service operates 24 hours a day and costs a flat $45 to anywhere on the island.

TRAIN

Coming from Malaysia by train, you'll disembark at **Tanjong Pagar Railway Station** (☎ 6222 5165) and may be set upon by taxi touts hoping to take advantage of the absence of a Changi-style controlled system. It's only a kilometre from here into Chinatown, 2km to the Colonial District and 3km to Little India, so the fare should not be more than $10 for the furthest trip. Insist the driver uses the meter or tell him to get lost.

BUS

Buses arriving from Malaysia drop you either at Lavender Bus Terminal (Map pp84–5, E4), Queen St Terminal (Map pp84–5, D6) or the Golden Mile Complex (p87), all of which are in poor locations

TAKE THE TRAIN

Travellers concerned with reducing their carbon footprint might consider reaching Singapore overland. Coming from the rest of Southeast Asia, there are train links pretty much all the way from Europe or China (with the exceptions of Cambodia and Laos). A train trip from Chiang Mai to Singapore in standard sleeper carriages only costs around US$80 and takes around three days.

in terms of late-night transport options. Calling a taxi is the best option (see p190).

BOAT

Coming from the Indonesian islands, you'll be disgorged at the **HarbourFront Ferry Terminal** (Map pp130-1, H6; ☎ 6513 2200; www.singaporecruise.com) or at the **Tanah Merah Ferry Terminal** (☎ 6513 2100; www.singaporecruise.com). From HarbourFront, it's a short walk to the HarbourFront MRT station, or there is a taxi rank outside. From Tanah Merah, catch bus 35 to either Bedok or Tanah Merah MRT stations, or catch a taxi.

VISAS

Visitors from the USA, UK, Australia, New Zealand, South Africa, Israel, most European countries and Asean member countries (except Myanmar) receive 30-day tourist visas on arrival by air. Citizens of the

Commonwealth of Independent States, Middle Eastern, African and South Asian countries require visas.

CUSTOMS

It's worth noting that visitors are forbidden from bringing cigarettes into Singapore, though in practice few people arriving at the airport are checked. First-time offenders are usually let off with confiscation and a warning.

The limit on alcohol is only 1L of duty-free wine, beer or spirits at the airport (and none if you're arriving from Malaysia or Indonesia), but you can bring as much cash

as you like! Take a letter from your doctor if you carry prescription medication.

Needless to say, it's insane to attempt to bring drugs into Singapore – and there are also strict punishments for bringing in firearms and pornography.

GETTING AROUND

Singapore has fantastic public transport – a tangled web of bus and MRT train routes taking you to the doorstep of most sights. The MRT is easy to navigate, but stops are sometimes far apart (walking in 35°C and high humidity is

Recommended Modes of Transport

	Orchard Rd	Chinatown	Colonial District & the Quays	Little India	Sentosa
Orchard Rd	-	MRT 10min	MRT 5min	MRT 15min	MRT, then monorail 25min
Chinatown	MRT 10min	–	MRT 10min	MRT 15min	MRT, then monorail 15min
Colonial District & the Quays	MRT 5min	MRT 10min	-	MRT 10min	MRT, then monorail 25min
Little India	MRT 15min	MRT 15min	MRT 15min	-	MRT, then monorail 25min
Sentosa	monorail, then MRT 25min	monorail, then MRT 15min	monorail, then MRT 25min	monorail, then MRT 25min	-
Eastern Singapore	bus 30min	bus 40min	bus 30min	bus 30min	bus, then monorail 45min
Holland Rd & Bukit Timah	bus 20min	bus 30min	bus 35min	bus 40min	bus 30min
Southwest Singapore	MRT 15min	MRT 5min	MRT 15min	MRT 15min	monorail 5min
Arab Quarter	MRT 10min	MRT 5min	MRT 3min	walk 10min	MRT, then monorail 25min
Jurong	MRT 25min	MRT 35min	MRT 30min	MRT 35min	MRT, then monorail 50min

sweaty work!), so it pays to brush up on those bus routes, which are usually clearly described at bus stops. Pick up a free MRT system map at any MRT station, or the *Bus Guide & Bus Stop Directory* ($3.90) from most bookshops. Due to car-ownership limitations, taxis are also considered public transport.

TRAVEL PASSES

There are two kinds of pass for Singapore public transport that save a whole lot of hassle buying tickets every time you travel.

Buy the Ez-link card from the customer service windows at MRT stations for $15, which includes a $5 nonrefundable deposit. It's good for use on all buses and trains and gives you cheaper fares. The cards can be topped up with cash or ATM cards at station ticket machines.

The **Singapore Tourist Pass** (www .thesingaporetouristpass.com) was finally resurrected after being abandoned for years. It offers unlimited travel on trains and most buses for $8 a day, plus discounts and offers at certain shops and restaurants.

MASS RAPID TRANSIT (MRT)

The ultraclean, safe and efficient Singapore **MRT** (☎ 1800 336 8900;

Eastern Singapore	Holland Rd & Bukit Timah	Southwest Singapore	Arab Quarter	Jurong
bus 30min	bus 20min	MRT 15min	MRT 10min	MRT 25min
bus 40min	bus 30min	MRT 5min	MRT 5min	MRT 35min
bus 30min	bus 35min	MRT 15min	MRT 3min	MRT 30min
bus 30min	bus 40min	MRT 15min	walk 10min	MRT 35min
monorail, then bus 45min	monorail, then bus 40min	monorail 5min	MRT, then monorail 25min	MRT, then monorail 50min
-	bus 45min	bus 35min	MRT or bus 10min	MRT, then bus 1hr
bus 45min	-	bus 30min	bus 40min	bus 35min
bus 35min	bus 30min	-	bus 30min	bus 35min
MRT or bus 10min	bus 40min	bus 30min	-	MRT 40min
MRT, then bus 1hr	bus 35min	bus 35min	MRT 40min	

www.smrt.com.sg) subway and light-rail system is the island's pride and joy – or one of them. It's the most comfortable and hassle-free way to get around, not least because it offers an escape from the heat.

Trains run from around 5.30am to just after midnight, departing every three to four minutes at peak times and every six to eight off-peak.

Fares range from $1.10 to $1.90, plus a $1 refundable deposit every time you buy a ticket. Buying an Ez-link card or Tourist Pass (see p189) makes life much easier.

Tickets are available at the automatic machines in stations, which take notes and give change, or from the customer-service windows.

BUS

Singapore's bus service should be the envy of the world. Clean and largely unvandalised, you rarely have to wait very long for one to turn up (but yes, sometimes two turn up at once) and they reach pretty much every corner of the island. Some even have TVs to entertain – or annoy – passengers!

Fares range from $0.90 to $1.80 (10% less with an Ez-link card). When you board the bus, drop the exact money in coins into the fare box (no change is given) or swipe your Ez-link card or Tourist Pass (see p189). Remember to swipe the card again when you get off.

For inquiries contact **SBS Transit** (☎ 1800 287 2727; www.sbstransit.com.sg).

Singapore Airlines runs the **SIA Hop-On** (☎ 9457 2896; www.siahopon.asiaone.com.sg) tourist bus, traversing the main tourist arteries every 30 minutes daily, starting at Raffles Blvd at 9am, with the last bus leaving at 5.30pm and arriving back at 7.35pm.

There's also a Sentosa Hop-On bus running between Raffles Blvd, Orchard Rd, Lau Pa Sat Festival Market and Sentosa. The first bus leaves Sentosa at 10am and the last at 5.30pm. Tickets cost $12/6 per adult/child, or $3 with a Singapore Airlines or Silk Air boarding pass or ticket. Buy tickets from the driver.

TAXI

The 'taxi issue' is one of Singapore's big unsolvable problems and a constant bugbear and conversation topic for city residents and the media. Sometimes they swarm like locusts, other times there are none, or drivers refuse to stop. Rain, peak hours, night times and shift-change times (which are unpredictable but usually occur between 4pm and 5pm) often render them impossible to find. Going out in the city at night could turn into a nightmare when it is time to come home.

The latest of many attempts to solve this problem initially appeared to make an impact, but it made taxis more expensive. Call-out charges, which once persuaded drivers in their hundreds to hide in back streets waiting to be booked, were lowered, while peak-hour charges and CBD surcharges were increased in an effort to lure drivers back into circulation.

Initially it worked, then the authorities decided to ban taxis from stopping anywhere except at designated taxi ranks in the city centre between 7am and 10pm, which has just made the situation a whole lot worse again (taxi ranks are few and far between and drivers don't often know where they are). It's bound to cause mass confusion, especially among visitors, so sense may prevail and hopefully it will be repealed.

The fare structure is enormously complicated, but basically taxis are metered and cost around $2.80 for the first kilometre, then $0.20 for each additional 385m. The average journey within the city centre will cost between $4 and $10, plus surcharges for phone and advance booking, peak-hour travel and CBD charges. Credit-card payments incur a 10% surcharge.

If you call a cab by phone, you'll be asked your name, location and destination. A message then tells you the licence plate number of your cab and the estimated arrival time. Taxi company numbers:
Comfort and CityCab CabLink ☎ 6552 1111

Premier Taxis ☎ 6363 6888
SMRT Cabs ☎ 6555 8888

PRACTICALITIES

BUSINESS HOURS

Shops generally open late and close late, so don't bother heading to Orchard Rd at 9am to beat the crowd – virtually nothing will be open until at least 10am, but shops will stay open until 9pm and often later.

Restaurants usually close between 2pm and 5pm, but hawker centres keep the woks on all day and often late into the night.

Government office hours are generally 9am to 6pm Monday to Friday, and 10am to 1pm on Saturday.

DISCOUNTS

Children receive up to 50% discounts at most tourist venues, sometimes gauged by how tall they are rather than by age. They can ride the MRT for free if they're under 90cm tall. Students with ID cards receive discounts at some venues.

ELECTRICITY

Electricity supply is reliable and runs at 220V to 240V and 50 cycles. Plugs are of the three-pronged, square-pin type used in the UK.

DIRECTORY

EMERGENCIES

Singapore has a very low crime rate and members of both sexes can walk around safely at any time of night. Pickpockets sometimes target tourists and the odd gang fight makes front-page news, but unless you go looking for it, trouble is unlikely to come looking for you. Don't import, take or sell drugs in Singapore or hang out with anyone who does – the death penalty awaits.

Ambulance/Fire ☎ 995
Police ☎ 999
SOS Helpline ☎ 1800 774 5935

Hospitals with 24-hour accident and emergency departments:
Gleneagles Hospital (Map pp40–1, C3; ☎ 6470 5688; 6A Napier Rd)
Mt Elizabeth Hospital (Map pp40–1, F3; ☎ 6731 2218; 3 Mt Elizabeth Rd)
Raffles Hospital (Map pp68–9, G2; ☎ 6311 1111; 585 North Bridge Rd)
Singapore General Hospital (Map pp52–3, B4; ☎ 6321 4113; Level 2, Block 1, Outram Rd)

HOLIDAYS

New Year's Day 1 January
Chinese New Year January/February (two days); date varies based on lunar calendar.
Good Friday April
Labour Day 1 May
Vesak Day May; varies.
National Day 9 August
Hari Raya Puasa October/November; date varies based on Islamic calendar.
Deepavali October; date varies according to the Indian almanac.

Christmas Day 25 December
Hari Raya Haji December/January; date varies based on Islamic calendar.

INTERNET

Most internet cafés in Singapore aren't actually cafés: plenty of computers, but no coffee. Many places are gaming centres filled with teenagers, so things can get raucous – hardly the space for that Skype call. Many hotels provide internet access (either in-room connections or business centres) and at Changi Airport there are dozens of free internet terminals.

Major internet service providers such as **CompuServe** (www.compuserve .com), **AOL** (www.aol.com) and **AT&T** (www .attbusiness.net) have dial-up nodes in Singapore. **SingTel** (www.singtel.com.sg) and **StarHub** (www.starhub.com) are the two biggest local providers.

Singapore has an ever-expanding network of around a thousand free wireless hotspots – and most cafés and pubs operate them. A list of hotspots can be found by following the Wireless@ sg link at www.info comm123.sg.

Some useful and interesting websites:
Changi International Airport (www .changi.airport.com.sg) Flight information and services at the world's favourite airport. Try to locate the free swimming pool.
Disgruntled Singaporean (disgruntledsin gaporean.blogspot.com) Series of articles and

musings from an opposition standpoint, plus links to other similarly dissenting blogs.

Mr Brown (www.mrbrown.com) Website of the blogger and podcaster Lee Kin Mun, who gained wider fame when his column in the *Today* newspaper was canned after he wrote rather too frankly about rising living costs in Singapore. The podcast, accessible through the website, is still popular.

Singapore Government (www.gov .sg) As you'd expect, very large and very comprehensive.

Singapore Tourism Board (www.visit singapore.com) Information on the city's top attractions, plus a useful events calendar.

Stomp (www.stomp.com.sg) Community site run by the official mouthpiece media company SPH, embodying the kind of carefully monitored 'open society' the government is trying to foster (pictures of people kissing in clubs, 'hot' teacher contests, but nothing too dangerous). For an insight into issues that preoccupy Singaporeans, check the 'Singapore Seen' section.

Uberture E-Mag (www.uberture.com) Nightlife, entertainment, shopping, society and pics of people smiling in nightclubs.

LANGUAGE

Singapore's official languages are Malay, Mandarin, Tamil and English.

Nearly everyone speaks Singapore's baffling English patois, known proudly as Singlish, which most visitors will find extremely hard to understand. Singlish is essentially an English dialect mixed with Hokkien, Malay and Tamil, spoken in a rapid, staccato fashion –

sentences are polished off with innumerable but essentially meaningless exclamatory words – *lah* is the most common, but you'll also hear *mah, lor, meh, leh, hor* and several others. (We once overheard a boy delivering the dubious romantic overture 'I love you hor' to his girlfriend.)

Fortunately for the bewildered visitor, most Singaporeans will instantly switch seamlessly into a more standardised English when they are speaking to foreigners, though if you have a strong accent yourself, don't be surprised if it's they who find you incomprehensible.

MONEY

If you use the MRT and buses, eat and drink at hawker centres and stay in budget accommodation, it's possible to get by in Singapore on less than $50 a day. Staying in a midrange hotel, eating in a mix of venues and doing some modest shopping will send your costs up above $200. Count on around $300 to $400 a day for a pleasantly indulgent stay. For exchange rates, see the Quick Reference (inside front cover).

NEWSPAPERS & MAGAZINES

The press in Singapore is theoretically free to assert its opinions, but in reality this is far from the case. Willing self-censorship combines with stern government oversight and complicit editors to keep dissent away from the pages of the local press. Any local journalist intent on breaching the unwritten boundaries known to the local media as 'OB markers' will not last long, as former columnist and current blogger Mr Brown found out (see Internet, p193).

The country's flagship paper is the feeble *Straits Times* broadsheet, which steers well clear of any issues that might cast the country in a negative light. The paper's coverage of Asia is not bad, though it's also skewed towards reinforcing national interests.

The tabloid *New Paper,* also a product of Singapore Press Holdings, offers up a lurid platter of crime, scandal, sensation and English football. Freesheet *Today* is the best read, but its status as a paper willing to test those OB markers has been lost.

International English-language publications such as *Time* and *Newsweek* are readily available, but you won't find the *Far Eastern Economic Review,* which has been banned and sued for daring to publish a story about opposition leader Chee Soon Juan.

For entertainment listings, see *8 Days, Time Out* or *I-S* magazines. Lifestyle magazines include *Her World* and *Expat Living.* Gourmands should check out *Tatler's Singapore's Best Restaurants* guide, while hawker food enthusiasts should buy the excellent *Makansutra* guidebook for an encyclopaedic rundown of the city's best street food, with a decent restaurant section as well.

ORGANISED TOURS

A number of companies offer tours that promise to reveal a different side to the city, or go into more depth about a certain aspect of Singapore culture. Some good ones:

Culinary Heritage Tour (☎ 6238 8488; www.eastwestplanners.com) Multiday tours immersing visitors in Singapore's food culture. Not for small appetites. Costs vary.

Imperial Cheng Ho Dinner Cruise (☎ 6533 9811; www.watertours.com.sg; daytime & dinner cruises adult $27-55, child $14-29) Cruises around Singapore waters in a hulking old replica of the *Cheng Ho* junk.

Original Singapore Walks (☎ 6325 1631; www.singaporewalks.com; adult/child from $25/15) Superb and deservedly popular series of offbeat guided walks through various parts of the city, including Chinatown, Little India and the quays, as well as WWII tours. No booking necessary, just check the website for meeting times and turn up.

Singapore DUCK Tours (☎ 6333 3825; www.ducktours.com.sg; adult/child $33/17) A bright yellow amphibious vehicle that tours the city streets before plunging into the harbour. We're including this because never again are you likely to have a chance to be so comprehensively embarrassed.

Singapore Zoo Management Tour
(☎ 6269 3411; www. zoo.com.sg; adult/child $20/10; 🕑 11am, 2pm & 4pm daily) Excellent behind-the-scenes tours of various exhibits with zoo staff. Fragile Forest at 11am, Reptile Garden at 2pm and baboons at 4pm.

TELEPHONE
Two cell-phone networks operate in Singapore, GSM900 and GSM1800, making it compatible with most of the rest of the world.

USEFUL PHONE NUMBERS
Local Directory Inquiries ☎ 100
International Direct Dial Code ☎ 0011
International Directory Inquiries ☎ 104
International Operator ☎ 1635
Singapore International Dial Code ☎ 65
Toll-free Tourist Hotline ☎ 1800 736 2000
Weather ☎ 6542 7788

TIPPING
Tipping is largely unnecessary and not expected in restaurants because of the 10% service charge automatically added to your bill. However some restaurants voluntarily omit the charge, possibly in the hope that it will improve the city's pretty dismal service culture. Funnily enough, it seems to work in many places.

Nobody tips in hawker centres.

TOURIST INFORMATION
Singapore Tourism Board (STB; ☎ 1800 736 2000; www.visitsingapore.com) pro-

vides the widest range of services, including tour bookings and event ticketing. There are visitors centres at the following locations (note Suntec City is an unmanned info desk).
Changi Airport (Terminals 1, 2 & 3; 🕑 6am-2am)
HarbourFront (Map pp130–1, H6; 01-31D, HarbourFront Centre; 🕑 10am-6pm)
Liang Court (Map pp68–9, C4; Level 1, Liang Court Shopping Centre, 177 River Valley Rd; 🕑 10am-10pm)
Little India (Map pp84–5, C6; The InnCrowd Backpackers, 73 Dunlop St; 🕑 10am-10pm)
Orchard Rd (Map pp40–1, F4; Cnr Cairnhill & Orchard Rds; 🕑 9.30am-10.30pm)
Suntec City (Map pp68–9, G4; Level 1, Suntec City, 3 Temasek Blvd; 🕑 10am-6pm)

TRAVELLERS WITH DISABILITIES
You'll find most major hotels, shopping malls and tourist attractions have good wheelchair access, but Little India's and Chinatown's crowded narrow footpaths will challenge anyone with mobility, sight or hearing issues. Taxis are plentiful, the MRT is wheelchair-friendly and Singaporeans are happy to help out. We've used the disabled icon to indicate venues with disabled access.

Access Singapore (www.dpa.org .sg) is a very useful guidebook for the disabled; it's available free from the website and STB offices (see left).

>INDEX

See also separate subindexes for See (p204), Shop (p205), Eat (p206), Drink (p207) and Play (p207).

000 map pages

SEE

000 map pages